WHEN MARX MEETS ISLAM

WHEN MARX MEETS ISLAM

NAVIGATING RADICAL IDEOLOGIES IN DEFENSE OF THE WEST

CRAIG CONSIDINE

PITCHSTONE PUBLISHING
DURHAM, NORTH CAROLINA

Pitchstone Publishing
Durham, North Carolina
www.pitchstonebooks.com

Library of Congress Cataloging in Publication Control Number: 2026024015

ISBN (paperback): 9781634312929
ISBN (ebook): 9781634312936

CONTENTS

PREFACE

Before diving into this book, it is important for me to define the terms Leftist and Islamist, which will appear often in the pages that follow. I am acutely aware that words are powerful and that even a slight reframing of a particular word can lead to miscommunication and misunderstanding. To avoid any confusion about what I mean by these terms, let me define them.

It is important to distinguish the term "liberal" from "Leftist." While the two terms are often conflated, classical liberalism is a political ideology linked to equality, individuality, and liberty. Liberals generally support capitalism, civil liberties, and freedom of speech. In contrast, Leftism is a political ideology that views capitalism and Western values as "oppressive" tools. It seeks to dismantle these existing systems, and its core tenets are linked to Marxism, which I will unpack throughout the entire book.

Similarly, there is a fundamental difference between "Muslims" and "Islamists." Muslims are people who practice their faith by following the Five Pillars of Islam, and many of them are peaceful and patriotic citizens. Islamists, on the contrary, are extremists who seek to impose their ideology on others. Many Islamists use extreme rhetoric, advocate for terrorism, and call for a global caliphate and sharia (Islamic law) on a national scale. They often use the West's own political and cultural systems to accomplish their radical agenda.

My criticism, in short, is not with liberalism, but rather with Leftism and its branches of "Marxism," "wokeism," and "progressivism." Similarly, I am not "anti-Muslim" or even "anti-Islam," as my published books and advocacy, mentioned throughout this book, demonstrate. Islamism, or political Islam, however, is an entirely different matter, and I have a problem with it because it—alongside its partner, Leftism—poses a significant threat specifically to the United States, Israel, and the West more broadly.

INTRODUCTION

LEFTISTS AND ISLAMISTS: A STRATEGIC CONVERGENCE

This book examines a dangerous strategic convergence—the growing alliance between Leftist revolutionaries and Islamist radicals. Building on David Horowitz's seminal 2004 work *Unholy Alliance—Radical Islam and the American Left*, I argue that what began as an ideological partnership has evolved into an active "soft war" against the West—especially the United States–Israel alliance. I use the terms "Leftist" and "Islamist" to be precise about the ideological nature of this alliance. These terms are not to be confused with classical liberals or ordinary Muslims, who are not the problem and, indeed, are often targets of this alliance. Rather, the alliance is composed of extremist ideologues who explicitly seek to dismantle Western institutions and impose radical alternatives that would supplant the West's democratic systems and liberal order. With those distinctions in mind, this book shows how the alliance operates today on campuses, in city streets, and inside institutions across the West.

Horowitz, a conservative author and former communist, provided initial insight into the convergence of Leftist and Islamist ideologies. He argued that this "unholy" alliance is rooted in Manichaeism, a third-century religion that divides the world into stark binaries such as good and evil and light and darkness. A similar black-and-white framework later appeared in the thought of the nineteenth-century German communist Karl Marx and remains evident in the rhetoric and actions of both Leftists and Islamists, who divide humanity into two groups: the "oppressed" and the "oppressors." As Horowitz argued, this all-or-nothing framework fosters a climate of anger, division, resentment, and victimhood, thus posing a direct threat to the West's civic culture and overall security.

While Horowitz warned of the threat that this "unholy alliance" posed, my argument is that a "soft war" has already begun between the Leftist-Islamist alliance and the West, and this war threatens the bedrock values of Western civilization. These include individual and personal liberties such as civic principles, democracy, Enlightenment rationalism, equal rights, freedom of conscience, freedom of expression, freedom of speech, individuality, open debate, religious freedom, and rule of law. Leftism and Islamism work synergistically against these ideals by exploiting the very tolerance and openness that Western values demand. Leftist promotion of diversity and multiculturalism provides ideological cover for Islamist norms to gain footholds, even as Islamist norms directly contradict Western values. The Leftist-Islamist alliance exploits the West's hard-fought freedoms to undermine the West from within, turning the tools of liberal democracies against its very own foundations. While I use the term "soft war" to make clear that the fight is still primarily over ideas and control of institutions, the potential consequences of losing the "soft war" for the West are devastating.

This battle has only grown and taken on new urgency since October 7, 2023. Although Israel is not geographically Western, it is certainly Western-aligned, if not functionally part of the West, due to its developed democracy and economy. For decades, the U.S.-Israel alliance has been a primary target of the Leftist-Islamist alliance. Still, Westerners as a whole largely understood the U.S.-Israel alliance to be one based on common interests and values. Following Hamas's attacks on Israel, this single issue—more than any other—has come to define the soft war, with its borders not just abutting but also sometimes overlapping with an active war. Further, thanks in large part to effective Leftist and Islamist social media campaigns, people across the political spectrum in the West—even among those well outside Leftist and Islamist circles—began to question whether the United States' alliance with Israel remains worth maintaining. A key talking point is that it is a "one-way" relationship in which U.S. taxpayer dollars flow to Israel with little return. In reality, the alliance is a genuine two-way strategic asset; it is one of the United States' most enduring and vital partnerships for several reasons.[1]

First, the U.S.-Israel alliance is rooted in shared democratic values. Israel stands as the only liberal democracy in the Middle East, upholding equal rights for all citizens, free elections, and the rule of law—including its significant Arab minority. In an era of rising authoritarianism worldwide, preserving democratic systems is essential, and supporting Israel reinforces America and the West's commitment to those principles.

Second, the alliance advances mutual security interests. Israel defends its democracy without requiring American troops on its soil, yet the partnership yields concrete benefits for the United States. Joint development of advanced systems such as Iron Dome, David's Sling, and Arrow missile defense has equipped both nations with superior capabilities against missile and rocket threats. Israel's intelligence sharing has also repeatedly thwarted terrorist plots targeting Americans and

1. Joseph Epstein, "Sorry, Israel-Haters—US Aid Pays Off Big for America and the Numbers Don't Lie," *New York Post*, April 25, 2026, nypost.com/2026/04/25/opinion/sorry-israel-haters-us-aid-pays-off-big-for-america/.

U.S. military bases in the Middle East,[2] directly enhancing U.S. national security.

Third, Israel's leadership and geopolitical position in the turbulent Middle East region also deliver lasting technological and economic advantages for Americans. Most of the $3.8 billion worth of aid from the United States to Israel must be spent on American-made military equipment. Israel's largest military equipment purchases flow to Lockheed Martin, Boeing, Raytheon, and General Dynamics, all key U.S. companies.[3] The F-35 program alone—which Israel was the first to use in combat—supports 290,000 American jobs, generates $72 billion in annual economic output, and has produced a $173 billion order backlog.[4]

Fourth, as a global hub of innovation, Israel contributes cutting-edge advancements in cybersecurity, electronic warfare, and counterterrorism that have been integrated into U.S. technological systems. Israel-based R&D centers for American companies like Google, Intel, and Microsoft drive breakthroughs in artificial intelligence, cybersecurity, and defense technology that keep America competitive and create jobs on U.S. soil. Beyond these security fields, Israeli firms are the second-largest source of foreign listings on NASDAQ, and Israeli investment in the United States has tripled to nearly $24 billion.[5] In New York alone, 600 Israeli-founded companies generated $19.5 billion in output in 2025 and supported 57,000 jobs. Bilateral trade between the two countries tops $49 billion.[6]

---

2. "Israeli Intelligence Helped Thwart Dozens of Terror Attacks Worldwide," *Haaretz*, September 28, 2017, www.haaretz.com/israel-news/2017-09-28/ty-article/israeli-intelligence-helped-thwart-dozens-of-terror-attacks-worldwide/0000017f-e110-d75c-a7ff-fd9dcaae0000.

3. Epstein, "Sorry, Israel-Haters."

4. Ibid.

5. Ibid.

6. Ibid.

To be clear, supporting Israel bolsters American innovation in critically important fields that will determine the fate of the twenty-first century. And for the West at large, supporting Israel safeguards shared democratic principles against authoritarianism and radical ideologies that threaten freedom of speech, religious liberty, and the rule of law. Israel's survival serves as a bulwark against anti-Western extremism; its fall would embolden jihadist groups, destabilize the Middle East, empower the West's adversaries, and signal weakness to the world. To put it bluntly, defending Israel is not an act of "Western charity," nor is it a sign that Western lawmakers have been "bought" or are acting as "puppets" of Jews or Israel itself—a tired accusation popular in Leftist circles and increasingly echoed in certain "woke right" quarters.[7] In reality, U.S. support of Israel is a hard strategic imperative that bolsters the West's resilience and security in an age of mounting authoritarian challenges from the likes of China, Iran, and Russia.

Given that the U.S.-Israel alliance serves as a central focus of the Leftist-Islamist alliance's attacks on Western civilization, a core argument of this book is that the U.S.-Israel alliance protects the very bedrock of Western civilization itself—with the United States serving as the West's undisputed leader and Israel acting as its forward sentinel, guarding the gates of the Mediterranean periphery of the Middle East and preventing the further westward spread of Islamism into Europe. While the book will necessarily refer to the wider situation playing out in the European Union—which, according to many scholars and experts, is already deeper into this "soft war" owing to its more advanced demographic crisis—the central strategic reality remains that the survival of the U.S.-Israel partnership is the decisive factor in whether the West ultimately prevails or succumbs.

---

7. Danny Burmawi, "How the Woke Right Joined the Left's War on Israel," *Times of Israel*, July 26, 2025, blogs.timesofisrael.com/how-the-woke-right-joined-the-lefts-war-on-israel/.

Within Western countries, the Leftist-Islamist alliance is not fighting a conventional war with tanks and missiles or even a guerrilla one with guns and bombs. Although there have been notable cases of Leftist-Islamist violence that have led to death and injury—along with many well-documented instances of physical intimidation and mob mobilization—the alliance has thus far largely been waging a "soft war"—a coordinated campaign of ideas, organizations, and narratives designed to erode Western values and undermine institutions from within. In pursuit of its goals, the alliance relies on five key components that work in concert, much like chess pieces that move together for attack. Using this chessboard analogy, the alliance's "pawns" are the students and activists who have limited mobility but can be promoted to stronger pieces. The "bishops" are professors who indoctrinate students with a specific ideology. The "knights" are organizations and networks that engage in strategic maneuvering and control societal narratives. The "rooks" are progressive politicians who can influence policy and legislation. And the most powerful pieces, the "kings" and "queens," are the international patrons who control resources and produce propaganda. While this analogy conveys the complex mechanics and key parts of the alliance, I will occasionally cite the works of George Orwell—specifically *Animal Farm* and *Nineteen Eighty-Four*—when discussing the alliance's modus operandi, such as its manipulation of language to control narratives and suppress dissent. Put simply, in the alliance's efforts to subvert Western values and institutions, it relies on Orwellian tactics.

THE DEADLY ALLIANCE: WHEN REVOLUTIONARY MARXISM MEETS ISLAMISM

As already noted, these are not merely theoretical concerns. In May 2025, I witnessed the deadly consequences of the Leftist-Islamist alliance firsthand while attending the annual policy conference of the

Middle East Forum (MEF) in Washington, D.C. During my panel, I discussed three sociological theorists aligned with the Leftist-Islamist alliance—Karl Marx, Antonio Gramsci, and Frantz Fanon. I explained that while Marx's classical view of "oppressed" and "oppressors" focused on the proletariat (the working class) and bourgeoisie (the elites), the collapse and inviability of communism in the late 1980s forced Leftists and Islamists to find a new "oppressed" group—minority groups in the West. Classical Marxism—focusing on class dynamics and economic issues—transformed into "cultural Marxism," focusing on multiculturalism and identity politics. Secondly, I discussed Gramsci, who viewed culture as the central site of inequality and advocated for "counter-hegemony" to instigate change from within society's existing systems. This Gramscian blueprint is used by Leftist and Islamist groups to break down Western institutions from within. Finally, I referenced Fanon, who endorsed violence as a "cleansing force" for the colonized to reclaim their self-respect. These three theories, I explained, have culminated in acts of extreme violence—and will continue to do so.

Tragically, events later that day provided evidence that we are no longer just talking about theory or history but about unprecedented events—the intentional targeting and assassination of Jews by Leftists in the United States, more raw proof that this Leftist-Islamist alliance and "soft war" against the West is real and intensifying. Hours after my panel, a young Israeli diplomat named Yaron Lischinsky, who had attended my session, and his fiancée, Sarah Milgrim, were murdered by Elias Rodriguez, a pro-Palestinian socialist, outside an event for young Jewish professionals and diplomats at the Capital Jewish Museum, just blocks from the MEF conference. Lischinsky and Milgrim advocated for interfaith coexistence and peace, which is the "kryptonite" of the Leftist-Islamist alliance, as I explain in later chapters. Rodriguez, the murderer, posted a manifesto titled "Escalate for Gaza, Bring the War Home," which justified violence as "political resistance" and called for an intifada (uprising) within the United States.[8] His online history was filled with pro-Hamas messaging and Marxist propaganda,[9] aligning him with Marxist groups like the Party for Socialism and Liberation (PSL) and Black Lives Matter.[10] Just one week after his act, twenty-eight Marxist organizations, including the "Free Elias Rodriguez Organizing Committee," rallied behind him, calling his actions a "legitimate act of resistance."[11] This incident encapsulates the core message of this book—that Marxism, as an ideological force, is being embraced by Islamists—and, in turn, that Marxists are embracing Islamists—to subvert Western civilization, dismantle American systems, and destroy Israel. The anti-Jewish violence on U.S. soil is not some random or isolated event. It is, rather, a manifestation of an intellectual framework that condemns capitalism and Western culture, promotes antisemitism, and targets Zionism as its ideological core.

The murders of Lischinsky and Milgrim sent shockwaves through the MEF conference, particularly for the Jewish Americans and Israelis in attendance. On the morning after their murders, my cell phone erupted with messages from Jewish friends, conveying a chilling sentiment: "It was only a matter of time before something like this happened," or more simply, "I am not surprised." Their responses touched on the fear

---

8. Ken Klippenstein, "The Israel Embassy Shooter Manifesto," *Ken Klippenstein*, May 22, 2025, www.kenklippenstein.com/p/the-israel-embassy-shooter-manifesto.

9. Eric Schorr, "The Eighth Front—DC Shooting Signals a New Phase in Israel's Global War," *Times of Israel*, May 23, 2025, blogs.timesofisrael.com/the-eighth-front-dc-shooting-signals-a-new-phase-in-israels-global-war/.

10. Mike Gonzalez, "Elias Rodriguez Is a Son of the Left's Revolutionary Ecosystem," Heritage Foundation, June 3, 2025, www.heritage.org/progressivism/commentary/elias-rodriguez-son-the-lefts-revolutionary-ecosystem.

11. Mathilda Heller, "Pro-Palestine, Marxist Groups Start 'Free Elias Rodriguez' Campaign, Laud 'Legitimate Act,'" *Jerusalem Post*, May 29, 2025, www.jpost.com/diaspora/antisemitism/article-855947.

that the antisemitic rhetoric was reaching a boiling point and was destined to erupt in violent acts by radicalized individuals like Rodriguez. This reality was further highlighted by my unsettling encounter at a Starbucks across the street from the conference hotel, where a Jewish American attendee told me, with resignation, "Now the violence is happening in America. The intifada is here." She voiced concerns about her safety and her family's future well-being, even considering emigrating to Israel. Despite being under attack by Hamas and other Iranian proxies at the time, Israel offered a perceived sanctuary from the domestic threat posed by Leftist and Islamist revolutionaries in the United States.

The chapters that follow will delve into the strategic alliance between Leftists and Islamists and their shared ideological enemy—namely, the West. The central argument is that the alliance is attacking the West's "civic culture," which has historically embraced democracy, Enlightenment values, and tolerance. This rights-based system stands in contrast to the aims of Leftists and Islamists, who seek social control through different means. Only by understanding this dynamic can we properly defend the West and its values. As philosopher Karl Popper argued, unlimited tolerance can ultimately empower the intolerant and lead to the destruction of a tolerant society. I will therefore conclude the book by offering insights into how to safeguard democratic principles against malicious actors who would exploit them for their own malign interests.

The West now stands at a critical crossroads. Only by understanding the nature of this "soft war"—and the five components driving it—can Westerners defend the vital U.S.-Israel alliance and, by extension, mount an effective defense of our civic culture and democratic values.

CHAPTER 1

CAMPUS RADICALS: THE FRONT LINES OF THE "SOFT WAR"

While sitting outside the Brochstein Pavilion on Rice University's campus in April 2025, I watched a Students for Justice in Palestine (SJP) protest unfold just yards away. SJP, the self-described "revolutionary" organization with more than 400 chapters across the United States and Canada,[1] has become notorious for disruptive tactics and calls for a "glo-

1. This figure comes from the National Students for Justice in Palestine (NSJP) organization, which offers some level of support to the chapters. National SJP, Instagram, www.instagram.com/nationalsjp/. Through its Linktree account (linktr.ee/nationalsjp), it offers a downloadable 85-page PDF titled *The University and the Reproduction of Capitalist-Imperialist Society* (Popular University Press, 2025) dedicated to "the Martyrs of Palestine, All Prisoners of Conscience and Action, and the Relentless Resistance of the People." The document's seven-point political program aims, among other things, to "transform the campus into . . . a platform for struggle, not a site of capitalist reproduction," and to "weaken the U.S. Empire from within its core." Prior to October 7, 2023, there were an estimated 250 chapters American Jewish Committee, "What Is Stu-

balized intifada." Many of its chapters have been suspended, banned, or placed on probation at universities across North America. That day, Rice demonstrators were rallying in support of Mahmoud Khalil, a former Columbia student detained by U.S. Immigration and Customs Enforcement (ICE) for serving as Hamas's "propaganda arm" in New York City.[2] Students in keffiyehs—the symbol of the Palestinian intifada—stood shoulder to shoulder with peers waving rainbow flags and other Leftist symbols. Their chants of "From the River to the Sea, Palestine Will Be Free" rang across the quad, a slogan widely understood as a call for Israel's destruction. For many of these protesters, Hamas's atrocities of October 7, 2023, were not acts of terrorism but a "legitimate reaction to oppression," reflecting the very victimhood narrative that binds the Leftist-Islamist alliance together.

These students are the foot soldiers—the pawns—of that alliance, wielding the power to disrupt campus life and assert their political will. The Rice protest was a microcosm of a much larger and more explosive movement that had already engulfed Columbia University. There, SJP-led encampments with fifty unauthorized tents led to three hundred arrests,[3] the cancellation of commencement ceremonies,[4] and a climate so

---

dents for Justice in Palestine, the Hamas-Supporting Anti-Israel Group Being Banned on College Campuses?," February 23, 2024, www.ajc.org/news/what-is-students-for-justice-in-palestine-the-hamas-supporting-anti-israel-group-being-banned.

2. Adam Kredo, "Columbia Activists, Including Mahmoud Khalil, Serve as Hamas's 'Propaganda Arm in New York City,' Lawsuit States," *Washington Free Beacon*, March 25, 2025, freebeacon.com/campus/columbia-activists-including-mahmoud-khalil-serve-as-hamass-propaganda-arm-in-new-york-city-lawsuit-states/.

3. Ayana Archie, "New York Police Arrest 300 People as They Clear Hamilton Hall at Columbia University," *NPR*, May 1, 2024, www.npr.org/2024/05/01/1248401802/columbia-university-protests-new-york.

4. Emily Forgash, "Columbia Commencement Ceremonies Canceled, School

hostile that a university rabbi advised Jewish students to "return home as soon as possible and remain home."[5] One activist, Khymani James, publicly declared that "Zionists don't deserve to live"[6] and compared them to Nazis and white supremacists.[7] James also drew inspiration from figures like Ghassan Kanafani, the Palestinian communist and former leader of the Popular Front for the Liberation of Palestine (PFLP), the Marxist revolutionary group long recognized by the U.S. government as a terrorist organization.[8] Kanafani, along with other PFLP leaders, orchestrated the Lod Airport massacre in Israel on May 30, 1972, which resulted in 26 deaths and 80 injuries. He believed that the Palestinian cause is a cause for every revolutionary, echoing Frantz Fanon's call for violence as a means to an end.

Another Columbia activist, Tarek Bazrouk, identified himself as a

---

Class Days Moved off Campus," *Columbia Spectator*, May 6, 2024, www.columbiaspectator.com/news/2024/05/06/columbia-commencement-ceremonies-canceled-school-class-days-moved-off-campus/.

5. Sarah Fortinsky, "Columbia University Classes Moved Online after Rabbi Says Jewish Students Should 'Return Home,'" *The Hill*, April 22, 2024, thehill.com/homenews/state-watch/4610826-columbia-university-classes-moved-online-rabbi-says-students-should-return-home/.

6. David Goldman, " 'Zionists Don't Deserve to Live,' Suspended Columbia Activist Said. Now His Group Rescinds Its Apology and Calls for Violence," *CNN*, October 9, 2024, www.cnn.com/2024/10/09/us/columbia-pro-palestine-group-apology.

7. Rebecca Cohen, "Columbia University Says It Has Banned Student Protestor Who Said 'Zionists Don't Deserve to Live,'" *NBC News*, April 26, 2024, www.nbcnews.com/news/us-news/columbia-university-says-banned-khymani-james-protester-said-zionists-rcna149642.

8. U.S. Department of State, "Foreign Terrorist Organizations," U.S. Department of State, n.d., www.state.gov/foreign-terrorist-organizations/.

"Jew hater,"[9] kicked a Jewish student in the stomach,[10] and sent texts threatening to "boom boom" any Jew he saw.[11] Federal prosecutors later charged him with hate crimes after discovering his phone contained pro-Hamas and pro-Hezbollah propaganda and messages from a chat group linked to Hamas's al-Qassam Brigades.[12] Being charged with federal hate crimes is the natural endpoint of the radical ideology that weaponizes Leftist and Islamist antisemitism.

A more recent development at my alma mater, American University, provides another real-time case that maps the theorists we will be exploring in this book. SJP had been suspended by American University officials in February 2026 for violations of university policies. The suspension stemmed from the university's investigation into a February 2025 SJP event titled "Debunking Zionist Lies Workshop." The graphic for the event featured an image of a person in a red and white keffiyeh holding a slingshot that read "Smash Zionism!"[13] SJP responded to the suspension by stating it "means nothing to us" and that "university repression will be met with resistance."[14] Through the SJP's Marxist lens, the university is regarded as part of the ideological superstructure that

---

9. U.S. Department of Justice, "New York Man Charged with Federal Hate Crimes After Repeatedly Assaulting Jewish Victims," U.S. Department of Justice—Office of Public Affairs, May 7, 2025, www.justice.gov/opa/pr/new-york-man-charged-federal-hate-crimes-after-repeatedly-assaulting-jewish-victims.
10. Ibid.
11. Megan Palin, "Columbia Protestor and Self-Proclaimed 'Jew Hater' Had Direct Link to Hamas' Terror Cell, Disturbing Phone Records Reveal—DOJ," *New York Post*, June 4, 2025, nypost.com/2025/06/04/us-news/protestor-tarek-bazrouk-had-link-to-hamas-militants-doj/.
12. Ibid.
13. Jerusalem News Syndicate Staff, "American University Suspends Students for Justice in Palestine Chapter," JNS.org, February 17, 2026, www.jns.org/u.s.-news/american-university-suspends-students-for-justice-in-palestine-chapter.
14. Ibid.

enforces the interests of the U.S.-Israel alliance. As a result, the disciplinary action was interpreted by the group as "repression" of the revolutionary axis that it wants to lead.

These U.S.-based protests are only a fraction of a much larger pattern impacting the West. Nearly identical scenes have played out on the European front, revealing the transnational nature of the Leftist-Islamist alliance. SJP's European counterparts—Samidoun: Palestinian Prisoner Solidarity Network and the Masar Badil Palestinian Alternative Revolutionary Path Movement—are both front groups for the PFLP. Mass pro-Palestinian protests and occupations at universities in France, Germany, and Belgium have seen similar encampments and disruptions, highlighting the alliance's global reach. One of the most controversial and disruptive European protests unfolded in May 2024 at the University of Amsterdam.[15] Students and activists occupied the school's Roeterseiland campus, erecting makeshift barricades from desks, bricks, wooden pallets, and bicycles. Protesters atop the barriers used fire extinguishers to repel advancing riot police, while others threw fireworks and blocked entrances. Dutch police eventually cleared the site using batons, tear gas, and even a bulldozer, resulting in dozens of arrests and widespread scenes of violence broadcast across Europe. Similarly, at a University of Vienna Library for Jewish Studies protest just a week after Hamas's October 7 massacre, students held signs with violent rhetoric like "Kill IsraHell."[16] In November 2023, Paris University's library was spray-painted with the slogans "Death to Israel, Death to the Jews" and "Death, Hell, Suits Them So Well."[17]

---

15. "Amsterdam pro-Palestinian Student Protest Broken Up by Police," *Reuters*, May 9, 2024, www.reuters.com/world/europe/pro-palestinian-protesters-occupy-amsterdam-university-overnight-local-media-2024-05-08/.
16. Michael Starr, "Rise of Antisemitism at European Universities," *Jerusalem Post*, August 28, 2025, www.jpost.com/diaspora/antisemitism/article-865510.
17. Ibid.

Like their American Jewish counterparts, many European Jewish students shared how unsafe they felt on university campuses, with one student explaining, "I wouldn't dare go to the campus with my Star of David necklace or in a generally Jewish recognizable way."[18] In both the United States and Europe, antisemitic rhetoric (e.g., calls for intifada and justifications for violence) is normalized, creating an unsafe environment not just for Jewish students but for all students, faculty, and staff.

The scenes on Western college campuses recall a phenomenon that Horowitz observed twenty years earlier during the anti-war protests against the 2003 U.S.-led invasion of Iraq. Horowitz noted that the Left's support for Islamist movements is a façade, allowing both sides to expand their networks and gain mainstream acceptance.[19] The absurdity of their convergence is striking, given that Leftists are typically pro-LGBTQ and secular, while Islamists are anti-LGBTQ and theocratic. Despite this, Leftists and Islamists have converged on a shared hatred of Israel and the United States, and members of both groups seek to undermine the liberal democratic order and impose their respective ideologies on the West.

LEGAL BATTLES: SJP, FARA, AND TERROR SPONSORSHIP

The stakes here are high and should not be underestimated. Antisemitic incidents on American campuses have surged dramatically in recent years, rising by about 400%[20] in the two weeks following October 7,

18. Ibid.

19. David Horowitz, *Unholy Alliance: Radical Islam and the American Left* (Washington, D.C.: Regnery Publishing, 2004), 127.

20. Kanishka Singh, "Over 70% of US Jewish College Students Exposed to Antisemitism This School Year, Survey Finds," *Reuters*, November 29, 2023, www.reuters.com/world/us/over-70-us-jewish-college-students-exposed-an-

2023. Meanwhile, according to one poll, 73% of Jewish college students reported experiencing or witnessing antisemitism on their campus in the 2023–2024 academic year.[21] The situation on British campuses is similarly concerning. Since Hamas's October 7 terrorist attack on Israel, antisemitic incidents at schools have remained at historically elevated levels. According to one study, a record 4,298 antisemitic incidents were recorded within the United Kingdom's education system in 2023. This fell to 3,556 incidents in 2024, but rose again by 4% in 2025 to 3,700—the second highest annual total ever.[22] The campus disruptions have not gone unanswered. Universities, Jewish students, and the families of victims are fighting back through the courts, turning the alliance's own tactics of disruption and intimidation against it. Still, these alarming statistics, coupled with the influence of "foot soldiers," demand immediate attention from education officials and Western lawmakers. The pawns of the alliance are creating a new reality where antisemitism is normalized.

A first-person account of a Jewish student at Columbia exposes SJP's disturbing support for Hamas's violent actions.[23] After hearing slogans calling for Israel's destruction, the Columbia student repeatedly attempted to engage with SJP members, only to be met with disregard for peaceful solutions. The student further argued that SJP's rhetoric fundamentally aligned with Hamas's charter and actively hindered the prospect of Palestinian self-determination, as well as a wider regional peace in the Middle East. SJP's rejection of peaceful dialogue directly

---

tisemitism-this-school-year-survey-2023-11-29/.

21. Ibid.

22. "Antisemitism in UK Schools Hit All-Time High over Last Three Years, Investigation Reveals," *Jerusalem Post*, April 5, 2026, www.jpost.com/diaspora/antisemitism/article-892108.

23. David Lederer, "Why I Counterprotest SJP rallies," *Columbia Spectator*, 7 March 2024, www.columbiaspectator.com/opinion/2024/03/08/why-i-counterprotest-sjp-rallies/.

contradicts the Western value of civil engagement, which is central to the health of a democracy's civic life. When this kind of intolerance is tolerated by universities like Columbia, the West's commitment to civility and pluralism erodes, and core Western values are replaced by the Orwellian principles of censorship and silencing, both of which are tactics of the Leftist-Islamist movement.

The rejection of peaceful dialogue follows a deliberate playbook, and it is worth noting that the pawns' movements are not organic. Instead, they are deliberate, strategic maneuvers. For example, a "toolkit" surfaced on SJP social media accounts just days after October 7.[24] This manual lauded Hamas's assault as a "historic win," explicitly endorsed "armed struggle," and served as a "how-to" guide for campus disruptions. While the "toolkit" did not explicitly reference Marxism, it undoubtedly reflected its violent, revolutionary essence. In addition to the "toolkit," SJP organized a "National Day of Resistance" just five days after October 7. This planned "resistance" included the glorification of terrorism and violence in Israel, including the targeting of children, the elderly, and other civilians killed in the attacks. A social media post surrounding this event laid responsibility for Palestinian deaths "solely on the Zionist entity," claiming Hamas's attack was "natural and justified."[25] Unfortunately, many college students—in their idealism and relative naiveté—had fallen victim to SJP's misleading and radical ideology.

SJP's extremism is not confined to disruptive actions and divisive

24. The Institute for the Study of Global Antisemitism and Policy, "National Students for Justice in Palestine (NSJP)," Institute for the Study of Global Antisemitism and Policy, 2024, www.congress.gov/118/meeting/house/117305/documents/HHRG-118-JU10-20240515-SD003.pdf.

25. American Jewish Committee, "What Is Students for Justice in Palestine, the Hamas-Supporting Anti-Israel Group Being Banned on College Campuses," American Jewish Committee, February 23, 2024, www.ajc.org/news/what-is-students-for-justice-in-palestine-the-hamas-supporting-anti-israel-group-being-banned.

rhetoric, as it is also the subject of legal scrutiny. A lawsuit filed in Virginia alleged that SJP-Columbia leaders had advance knowledge of the October 7 attack and responded in real time with a coordinated propaganda campaign, fueled by the toolkit.[26] The lawsuit states that "Three minutes before Hamas began its attack on that day, Columbia SJP posted on Instagram 'We are back!!'" Families of American victims have claimed that SJP violated the Foreign Agents Registration Act (FARA), a law requiring agents of foreign actors engaged in political activities to disclose their relationships with foreign actors, by receiving funding from foreign entities and openly supporting Hamas's actions. Attorneys have echoed these concerns, labeling SJP as "Hamas's agents of chaos in the United States."[27] These allegations raise serious questions about SJP's compliance with U.S. laws and its role in promoting radical ideologies on college campuses.

The legal pressure on SJP is mounting on several fronts. Separate legal cases raise additional alarms about the group's actions. One lawsuit against 40 anti-Israel agitators, filed by two Columbia custodians, relates to events at the school's Hamilton Hall in April 2024, when pro-Palestinian protesters occupied the building.[28] The two custodians claimed that the agitators held them hostage, committed battery and assault against them, and conspired to violate their civil rights.[29] In another

---

26. Jesus Mesa, "Columbia Activists Had Prior Knowledge of Bombshell Lawsuit Claims," *Newsweek*, March 25, 2025, www.newsweek.com/columbia-activists-had-prior-knowledge-oct-7-bombshell-lawsuit-claims-2050296.

27. Ariel Kahana, "Bereaved US families Call for Probe of 'Students for Justice in Palestine,'" *Jerusalem News Syndicate*, August 2024, www.jns.org/bereaved-us-families-call-for-probe-of-students-for-justice-in-palestine/.

28. Adam Sabes, "Columbia University Janitors Sue Anti-Israel Agitators Accused of Holding Them Hostage in Campus Building," Fox News, April 29, 2025, www.foxnews.com/us/columbia-university-janitors-sue-anti-israel-agitators-accused-holding-them-hostage-campus-building.

29. Mathilda Heller, "Columbia Suspends, Expels and Revokes Degrees of over

case, the New York State Supreme Court upheld Columbia's suspension of its SJP chapter for repeated policy violations, claiming that there is no evidence to support SJP's assertion that it is unfairly singled out for punishment based on its "pro-Palestinian" position.[30] The New York Civil Liberties Union (NYCLU), in defense of SJP, used an Orwellian tactic, accusing Columbia of the very censorship SJP was being criticized for.[31] This form of propaganda is designed to deflect blame, maintain control, and confuse the public. SJP in the United States and its counterpart organizations in Europe appear to have achieved just that.

In summary, the pawns of the Leftist-Islamist alliance are discovering that their actions carry legal consequences. While they continue to test the boundaries of free speech, universities and courts are beginning to draw clear distinctions between protected protest and unlawful harassment or even material support for terrorist groups. This legal pushback is worth keeping an eye on, as it sets the stage for a broader struggle over who controls the ideological battlefield in higher education.

CAMPUS CONFRONTATIONS: SJP RHETORIC AND ITS MARXIST FOREBEARS

My time at Rice had been academically tranquil until 2020, when the COVID-19 pandemic and the Black Lives Matter (BLM) movement intensified the "cultural Marxism" turn in academia. Learning spaces be-

---

70 Pro-Palestine Protesters," *Jerusalem Post*, July 28, 2025, www.jpost.com/diaspora/antisemitism/article-862484.

30. Emily Pickering, "New York State Supreme Court Upholds Columbia's suspension of SJP and JVP," *Columbia Spectator*, November 13, 2024, www.columbiaspectator.com/news/2024/11/13/new-york-state-supreme-court-upholds-columbias-suspension-of-sjp-and-jvp/.

31. New York Civil Liberties Union, X, post dated November 8, 2024, x.com/NYCLU/status/1854924491220009114.

came ideological battlegrounds where the pursuit of truth often ceded to identity politics. I experienced this firsthand in 2024 when I organized a screening of the documentary film *October 8*,which examined the rise of antisemitism on college campuses since the Hamas attack.[32] The Rice-SJP chapter responded by calling the event "deeply troubling normalization of propaganda for the genocidal Israeli state."[33] Its critique was a living example of Marxism, pitting "oppressed" Palestinian voices against the "oppressor"—the Israeli state and its supporters. Personally, it was ironic to be accused of "promoting genocidal violence" by a group that seems to overlook how its actual, stated goals are similar to Hamas, which, according to its own manifestos, advocates for the full destruction of Israel.[34] Perhaps, in its pursuit of "anti-imperialist perspectives," Rice-SJP has developed a rather selective definition of violence and genocide, one that conveniently omits the very real and well-documented actions of those they champion. For instance, a scholarly analysis based on the Genocide Convention concluded that Hamas's October 7 attack on Israel constituted genocide, arguing that Hamas's actions met both the physical element and specific intent requirements for genocide, as evidenced by Hamas's ideology, systematic policies, and leadership statements.[35]

---

32. Kat Cosley Trigg, "Understanding the Unthinkable—'October 8' sSreening Sparks Reflection at Rice," *Rice University News and Media Relations*, May 5, 2025, news.rice.edu/news/2025/understanding-unthinkable-october-8-screening-sparks-reflection-rice.

33. Rice University Students for Justice in Palestine, "Tuesday's Screening of the Film October 8 at Rice University," April 17, 2025, www.instagram.com/p/DIjVs4KAeta/?hl=en&img_index=1.

34. Wilson Center, "Doctrine of Hamas," October 20, 2023, www.wilsoncenter.org/article/doctrine-hamas.

35. Avraham Russell Shalev, "Hamas' October 7th Genocide—Legal Analysis and the Weaponisation of Reverse Accusations—A Study in Modern Genocide Recognition and Denial," *Israel Law Review*, www.cambridge.org/core/

Another encounter with Rice-SJP occurred in June 2025 when I organized the "Woman Life Freedom" mural at Rice.[36] The mural, created by Iranian-American and Christian activist Hooman Khalili, honored two women—Mahsa Amini, a Kurdish Iranian woman killed by Iran's "morality police" for refusing to wear the hijab, and Shirel Haim-Pour, an Iranian Jewish soldier killed on October 7. I collaborated on this mural with my colleague, Moshe Vardi, a distinguished professor of mathematics at Rice. Rice-SJP responded by calling the mural "Zionist propaganda at Rice," "deeply racist," and "Islamophobic," and claimed that Vardi and I were "Zionist faculty"—a label neither of us refutes, given our support for the Jewish people's connection to their ancestral homeland.[37] This attack reveals that the group's campus operations are not simply about activism but rather are an extension of a Marxist framework that embraces revolutionary "resistance," demonizes opponents, and spreads propaganda for Islamist groups like Hamas.

If it is not clear by now, campuses have indeed become the battleground of the "soft war" against truth and Western values—attacks that Vardi has worked to counter.

---

journals/israel-law-review/article/hamas-october-7th-genocide-legal-analysis-and-the-weaponisation-of-reverse-accusations-a-study-in-modern-genocide-recognition-and-denial/322198E636341BE82F37ED7147FEB0F5.

36. Sam Byrd, "Internationally Recognized 'Woman Life Freedom' Mural Makes US Debut at Rice," *Rice University News and Media Relations*, June 18, 2025, news.rice.edu/news/2025/internationally-recognized-woman-life-freedom-mural-makes-us-debut-rice.

37. Rice University Students for Justice in Palestine, "We Condemn Zionist Propaganda at Rice," Rice University Students for Justice in Palestine, June 6, 2025, www.instagram.com/p/DKkKOaSAYBX/?hl=en&img_index=1.

COUNTERING THE "MORAL ROT": PRO-ISRAEL VOICES ON COLLEGE CAMPUSES

Moshe Vardi has been a leading voice in exposing antisemitism at Rice, which he calls "Israelophobia."[38] As a second-generation Holocaust survivor and a dual citizen of the United States and Israel, he brings a unique perspective to his advocacy. Our collaboration on events has given me insight into the ideological battles being waged by the "foot soldiers" of the Leftist-Islamist alliance. His perspective is rooted in Julien Benda's 1927 book, *La Trahison des Clercs* ("The Treason of the Intellectuals"), and he argues that American academics have descended into antisemitism, much like their European counterparts in the 1920s.[39] His documentation of antisemitism at Rice and the university's response has brought to light several alarming incidents.

In October of 2022, a group of Rice students attempted to establish Students Supporting Israel (SSI), a national student group advocating for Israel, as a counterpoint to the growing activities of Rice-SJP. Vardi agreed to sponsor the club; however, SSI's original application faced resistance. Rice's Student Association (SA) rejected the club's petition, citing its "strong political nature focused on a contentious topic."[40] This initial rejection, which only reversed after Vardi's intervention, highlights the subtle yet significant student biases that obstruct pro-Israel voices on campuses and effectively serve the aims of Leftists and Islamists who seek to silence counternarratives.

The nature of the Leftist-Islamist alignment at Rice was further exposed a year later, in September of 2023, when Rice Pride, an LGBTQ

---

38. Moshe Vardi, "Antisemitism, Anti-Zionism, Israelophobia, and the U.S. Civil-Rights Act," *Medium*, June 16, 2024, medium.com/@vardi/antisemitism-anti-zionism-israelophobia-and-the-us-civil-rights-act-5d7fcbfec0b7.
39. Moshe Vardi, "A Moral Rot at Rice University," *Medium*, December 6, 2023, medium.com/@vardi/a-moral-rot-at-rice-university-86440aede302.
40. Ibid.

student group, severed ties with Houston Hillel, the local chapter of the largest Jewish campus organization in the world, which had supported LGBTQ students at Rice for years. Houston Hillel was deemed "intolerant" by Rice Pride because Hillel International prohibited its chapters from partnering with groups that advocate for a boycott of Israel or deny Israel's right to exist, which Rice Pride apparently does. Rice Pride decided to sever ties with Rice's most important Jewish student organization in the name of "inclusion." The irony here is palpable, as Vardi noted, because "Israel is the only country in the Middle East with solid LGBTQ rights."[41] Yet, it is targeted by those claiming to champion diversity and cynically manipulating identity politics.

These cases provided a precursor to the intensifying ideological battles that would soon engulf the campus. Weeks after October 7, a faculty petition circulated in Rice's Schools of Humanities and Social Sciences. This petition dedicated a mere eleven words to mourning Jewish and Israeli lives lost, while the remaining 1,100 words focused on expressing "solidarity with the people of Palestine in their struggle for liberation." To eliminate any ambiguity, Israel was referred to as the "Israeli Zionist state." The 240 hostages held by Hamas were not mentioned at all in the statement. The petition's signatories, identifying as scholars of "Blackness, Indigeneity, Latinidad, state violence, colonialism, human rights, anti-imperialism, social movements, queerness, transness, gender, disability, critical media anthropology, and visual culture," offered an extraordinary collection of Leftist buzzwords.[42] Such academic terms serve to legitimize the binary of "oppressed" versus "oppressor," the Marxist worldview that provides the intellectual scaffolding for anti-Zionism and the broader ideological war against Western values.

Following the faculty statement, the ideological tide continued to swell as campus organizations amplified the anti-Zionist narrative. Two

41. Ibid.
42. Ibid.

months after the faculty petition was published, the Rice SA Senate affirmed its support for the statement, again omitting any mention of the October 7 attack. The resolution called on Rice's president to "affirm its commitment to a culture of care for our Palestinian, Arab, and Muslim student body, faculty, staff, and community." Jewish students were omitted. As Vardi observed, "Apparently, Jews do not deserve a culture of care." Again, the selective concern for "care" and "solidarity" exposes the ideological underpinnings of the Leftist-Islamist alliance, which dehumanizes Jews and Israelis to advance its anti-Zionist and anti-American agenda.

Vardi's work in exposing antisemitism at Rice and his role in establishing the SSI have opened up opportunities for me to collaborate with the club. In the fall semester of 2024, the SSI invited me to speak at its 9/11 commemoration event on campus. The event, which included city officials and law enforcement, aimed to unite the campus in a shared commitment to civility and opposition to terrorism. One student leader said the purpose of the event was to "honor the victims of the attacks and to unite the Rice campus under principles of anti-terrorism."[43] The commemoration concluded with a visual tribute. Attendees and speakers collectively placed small American flags in a 9/11 formation in front of the university's flagpole to honor the fallen. This act of remembrance, rooted in patriotism, is antithetical to the Leftist-Islamist agenda, which typically associates patriotism with "opposing one's country rather than supporting it."[44] Our focus on preventing the normalization of terrorism, a key objective of the "foot soldiers" who defend and praise Hamas, was a central message of the event. We demonstrated that even on campuses facing radical ideological pressures from students and activists, there are

---

43. Jewish Herald-Voice, "Rice 'Students Supporting Israel' Holds 9/11 Commemoration," *Jewish Herald-Voice*, September 26, 2024, jhvonline.com/rice-students-supporting-israel-holds-commemoration-p33993-281.htm.

44. Horowitz, *Unholy Alliance*, 83.

concerted efforts to promote a clear stance against extremism. Our collective actions, standing for truth and shared values, offer a counterpoint to the Marxist worldview of the Leftist-Islamist alliance, which is fueled by the forces of division and ideological subversion.

THE WOKE THOUGHT POLICE: SILENCING DISSENT IN ACADEMIA

George Orwell's depiction of the "Thought Police" in *Nineteen Eighty-Four* serves as a warning about the tactics used by students to silence dissent in academia. In Orwell's vision, this secret force existed to detect and punish "thoughtcrime," or any idea deemed "unorthodox" or "disloyal" to the ruling Inner Party. Its methods involved cultivating psychological manipulation and fear, demanding ideological conformity through surveillance, speech codes, and reporting systems designed to trigger investigations and disciplinary actions based on perceived "harmful" speech. This apparatus worked in *Nineteen Eighty-Four* to eliminate rebellion by eradicating independence and critical thought before it could be openly expressed, fostering a climate of paranoia and self-censorship. While fictional, the ideological policing in Orwell's book mirrors contemporary academic environments, where the boundaries of acceptable discourse are enforced, and the cost of intellectual unorthodoxy can be severe for those who dare to challenge hegemonic narratives.

Another colleague and friend, Timothy Jackson, a Jewish music professor at the University of North Texas (UNT), faced such an ordeal. In 2019, he found himself at the center of a controversy involving accusations of racism and attempts at censorship. The controversy began when Jackson penned a response in the *Journal of Schenkerian Studies* to Philip Ewell, an African American scholar of classical music, who had criticized Heinrich Schenker, the influential twentieth-century Jewish music theorist, for his alleged history of "white supremacism."[45] According to Jackson, Ewell's characterization of Schenker went beyond "historiography"; it hit at "the integrity of scholarly inquiry itself—the pursuit of truth and historical accuracy," as well as the dangers of ideological rigidity that Orwell warned about.[46]

The Jackson-Ewell disagreement escalated into ideological policing. Following the publication of his rebuttal, Jackson was met with a mob of students clamoring for his removal. Students involved with the *Journal of Schenkerian Studies*, which Jackson founded and edited, released a public statement condemning Jackson's rebuttal as "racist" and expressing "solidarity" with Ewell's efforts to "address systematic racism in and beyond the field of music theory."[47] The students' statement went further, calling for a complete systematic overhaul, a tactic from Marx's revolutionary playbook. This behavior, which one writer aptly termed "herd calling," involves attacking professors merely for upsetting "irritable 'progressives' on campus." In effect, it is a form of "thought policing" that enforces dominant Leftist orthodoxy in Western academia and punishes those who deviate from it.

The push to penalize dissenting voices like Jackson was not limited to the student body. A group of faculty members from the UNT music department released its own public statement echoing the sentiments of the "foot soldiers."[48] Jackson's colleagues asserted their "solidarity"

45. Norman Lebrecht, "A Cancelled Music Professor Speaks Out," *Slippedisc*, August 4, 2020, slippedisc.com/2020/08/a-cancelled-music-professor-speaks-out/.

46. Ibid.

47. Jack Horrigan, "UNT Professor Sues after Controversial Article Results in His Removal as Journal Head," Free Speech Project, April 23, 2021, freespeechproject.georgetown.edu/tracker-entries/university-of-north-texas-sued-over-alleged-free-speech-violation/.

48. Stephen Stuempfle, "Statement of UNT Faculty on Journal of Schenkerian Studies," *The Society for Ethnomusicology*, July 31, 2020, www.ethnomusicolo-

with the students, claiming that Jackson's response to Ewell was "replete with racial stereotyping and tropes," further accusing the journal itself of fostering "racist discourse."[49] In response to these accusations, Jackson highlighted his personal history of promoting and mentoring people of color globally, as well as his consistent support for initiatives that foster appreciation for classical music among diverse communities in Western society. UNT, nevertheless, succumbed to the pressure, launched an investigation, halted the journal's publication, and cut off its funding.

Sensing that his First Amendment rights had been violated and that he had been defamed, Jackson filed a lawsuit against the university and eighteen individual defendants. His case garnered significant media attention, including coverage in the *New York Times*.[50] Jackson's lawyers alleged that the university applied a "double standard," criticizing his journal for publishing an anonymous author while overlooking the same practice in *Theoria*, another UNT College of Music journal. In January 2024, a judge ruled against the university's request to dismiss the case, finding that Jackson had successfully demonstrated a plausible First Amendment violation.[51]

As a Legal Insurrection article observed, this case encapsulates the

---

gy.org/news/519784/Statement-of-UNT-Faculty-on-Journal-of-Schenkerian-Studies.htm.

49. Ayden Runnels, "From Racism Claims to a $725,000 Settlement, a UNT Professor's Lawsuit Mirrors Texas' Shifting Views on Free Speech," *The Texas Tribune*, July 30, 2025, www.texastribune.org/2025/07/30/texas-unt-free-speech-lawsuit-timothy-jackson/.

50. Michael Powell, "Obscure Musicology Journal Sparks Battles over Race and Speech," *The New York Times*, February 14, 2021, www.nytimes.com/2021/02/14/arts/musicology-journal-race-free-speech.html.

51. Jillian Nachtigal, "Professor Who Sued University Has Preliminary Win in Court," *North Texas Daily*, April 13, 2024, www.ntdaily.com/news/professor-who-sued-university-has-preliminary-win-in-court/article_063a9e48-fd98-5bf9-ad45-c5471163f2c9.html.

phenomenon of "woke" dominance on Western college campuses, where dissenters are targeted much as members of tribes attack others from an enemy tribe.[52] The prevailing philosophy among students, activists, and professors is not "live and let live," but rather, "agree with us or suffer," highlighting how scholarly argument, which has historically been typical in the Western world, is no longer welcome when it comes to challenging Leftist narratives. This targeting of those who do not conform to ideological purity tests, reminiscent of the Inner Party's tactics, is a troubling parallel to methods employed by the Leftist-Islamist alliance. For intellectual purposes, it is also worth comparing "woke" strategies, like the ones we see here, to traditional religious values. "Wokeism," as the British Anglican priest and theologian Nigel John Biggar astutely pointed out, "borrows Christianity's language of oppression and redemption, but sheds the humility that knows one's own fallibility and sin. So it does not listen, does not reflect, and does not correct itself. It smears, misreports, intimidates, and calls that righteousness."[53]

Jackson's predicament, now a widely discussed legal case, illustrates how the contemporary obsession with "white supremacy" among the "foot soldiers" can lead to the silencing of dissenting voices and the targeting of individuals who deviate from what some perceive as "woke orthodoxy." These students, acting as pawns, are a force of censorship on the ideological battlefield.

---

52. Mike La Chance, "The Woke Mob in Academia Is Coming for Music Too," *Legal Insurrection*, December 19, 2023, legalinsurrection.com/2023/12/the-woke-mob-in-academia-is-coming-for-music-too/.

53. Nigel Biggar, "Wokeness Is Christian Heresy," *Biggar Picture* (Substack), April 20, 2026, www.nigelbiggar.co.uk/p/wokeness-is-christian-heresy.

CAMPUS AS A BATTLEGROUND: A PRELUDE TO THE ACADEMIC BATTLEFIELD

This opening chapter has shown that student activists serve as the "foot soldiers" of the Leftist-Islamist alliance. Without their energy on the ground, the movement would stall. Yet, their actions are neither spontaneous nor isolated. They are the visible tip of a much larger ideological campaign being waged against the West. Our next battlefield is the classroom.

CHAPTER 2

ACADEMIA UNDER SIEGE: CULTURAL MARXISM IN UNIVERSITY CURRICULA

As we move from the "foot soldiers" on the front lines to the professors who arm them, we enter the second major battlefield of the soft war—the university curriculum. Here, the alliance's "bishops"—the professors who shape what students learn and how they perceive the world—"recruit" and "train" the next generation of pawns. This chapter examines how cultural Marxism, Critical Race Theory, social justice ideology, Gramsci's cultural hegemony and "war of position," Fanon's celebration of violence, and Edward Said's Orientalism have been woven into the classroom, giving intellectual legitimacy to the Leftist-Islamist alliance.

MARXISM'S NEW FRONTIER: THE CULTURE WARS ON CAMPUSES

The Trojan Horse metaphor is an apt way to frame this chapter on ideological indoctrination. The story of the Trojan Horse comes from Greek mythology and describes events said to have occurred during the Trojan War of the thirteenth century BCE. It is briefly referenced in the *Odyssey*, the epic poem by Homer written many centuries later, and more fully described in Virgil's *The Aeneid,* written more than a millennium later. During the war, the Greeks were unable to conquer Troy by conventional means, so Odysseus, the king of Ithaca, devised a plan to build a colossal wooden horse as an offering to Athena, the Greek goddess. The Greeks left the wooden horse outside the gates of Troy and pretended to sail away, leaving only Sinon, a Greek, to convince the Trojans of their sacred offering. The Trojans pulled the horse into their city, but later that night, while the Trojans slept, the Greek soldiers hiding inside the horse emerged within Troy's walls. The soldiers opened the Trojan gates, allowing the rest of the Greek army, which had never sailed away, to enter. Troy was subsequently sacked, and the Greeks emerged victorious in the war.

Critics argue that "cultural Marxism" has acted like a Trojan Horse in Western societies, largely due to the Frankfurt School, a German academic group that applied Marx's theories in the 1920s and 1930s. The Frankfurt School was primarily critical of "mass culture," describing it as a weapon used by the "elites" to control and oppress people. Two academics of the group, Max Horkheimer and Theodor W. Adorno, believed that culture, not economics, was the primary tool for maintaining capitalist power.[1] This "cultural turn" away from Marx's class-based grievances shifted the focus of socialists and communists from fighting capitalism to fighting Western values like individualism, meritocracy, and patriotism.

Building on this critique of Western culture, Herbert Marcuse, another member of the Frankfurt School, became a key figure in "cultural Marxism." He argued that revolutionaries would not be the working

1. Internet Encyclopedia of Philosophy, "The Frankfurt School and Critical Theory," *Internet Encyclopedia of Philosophy*, n.d., iep.utm.edu/critical-theory-frankfurt-school/

class, but rather, individuals "marginalized" by society because of their race and ethnicity, making them the most motivated to radically transform society.[2] By 1989, as journalist Felicity Barringer noted in her *New York Times* article, "The Mainstreaming of Marxism in U.S. Colleges," "cultural Marxism" was deeply entrenched within academic institutions.[3] This transformation proved critical in facilitating alliances between Leftist and Islamist groups, who collectively framed their struggles in terms of oppression from and resistance against Western powers.

The European-originated ideological shift to cultural Marxism has inevitably seeped into European universities and fueled campus radicalism. One scholar described the current situation in European universities as one of "institutionalized socialism," in which institutions have become largely detached from rigorous scientific research and empirical fact-finding.[4] The scholar noted that "the social consciousness is much more to the left" than in the United States and that "productivity and accomplishment are generally regarded with suspicion."[5] This characterization reveals a deeper anti-Western sentiment permeating Western academia. By framing success and merit as "suspect"—often recast as tools for "oppression" or "capitalist hegemony"—the dominant ideology dismisses the very foundations of Western civilization—individualism, rational inquiry, and the pursuit of truth.

This pervasive anti-Western ideology in academia mirrors the subversive process that Yuri Bezmenov, a former Soviet intelligence officer

---

2. Julian Eagles, "The Situationists, Marcuse and the 'Great Refusal' of the 'Hopeless Cases'—The Socially Marginalized, Rebellion and Revolution," *International Critical Thought*, 2017, 2.

3. Felicity Barringer, "Education; The Mainstreaming of Marxism in U.S. Colleges," *New York Times*, October 25, 1989, www.nytimes.com/1989/10/25/us/education-the-mainstreaming-of-marxism-in-us-colleges.html.

4. Henrique Schneider, "Elite Universities: A Radical Left hotbed," *GIS Reports Online*, August 16, 2024, www.gisreportsonline.com/r/universities-radical-left/.

5. Ibid.

who defected to the United States, described in a 1984 interview. During it, he warned of his former country's four-stage strategy to subvert the West: "demoralization," "destabilization," "crisis," and "normalization."[6] Bezmenov claimed that the "demoralization" stage—a "great brainwashing"—was already complete by 1984. He pointed to the "hippie" counterculture of the 1960s as evidence that Americans were "contaminated" by Marxist ideas. His warnings are still relevant today, as a generation of "new hippies" is being influenced by the Leftist-Islamist alliance within academic departments across the West.

The rise of "cultural Marxism" in academia has had a profound impact on the intellectual landscape of Western universities. The new generation of Marxists focuses on wielding power *within* institutions rather than dismantling them from the outside. They seek to control the means of "meaning production" by controlling academic departments, discourse, and journals.[7] Their influence within academia allows them to shape the minds of future generations, indoctrinating students with ideologies that promote narratives that threaten the United States, the broader West, and Israel. This, ultimately, is the bishop's move—capture the minds of university students from a position of authority and influence.

CRITICAL RACE THEORY AND THE WEAPONIZATION OF SOCIAL JUSTICE

A noticeable obsession with race and racism has permeated universi-

---

6. Yuri Bezmenov, "1984 Interview Between G. Edward Griffin and Yuri Bezmenov," *Fish Eaters*, n.d., www.fisheaters.com/srpdf/bezmenovinterview.pdf.

7. Mike Gonzalez and Katharine Gorka, "How Cultural Marxism Threatens the United States—and How Americans Can Fight It," *Heritage Foundation*, November 14, 2022, www.heritage.org/progressivism/report/how-cultural-marxism-threatens-the-united-states-and-how-americans-can-fight.

ty campuses in recent years. As a professor, I must constantly navigate race-related issues, fearing accusations of promoting "whiteness" and "white supremacy" or failing to adequately promote collective "white guilt." Conversations in the classroom, regardless of my efforts to make them constructive, often devolve into assigning blame to white people. If a white student excels, it is attributed to "white privilege." Conversely, if a black or brown student underperforms, the professor is deemed insufficient in addressing "white privilege." This environment is paralyzing. We now live in an era where students, influenced by their pre-college programming and exposure to radical information, like that seen on TikTok, perceive race and racism in every facet of existence in the West.

How did we arrive at this juncture, and what are the implications of this transformation? The answer, in part, lies in the influence of Critical Race Theory (CRT).[8] Derived from "critical theory," an academic concept and intellectual movement pioneered by Max Horkheimer, the German sociologist, CRT is a conceptual framework for analyzing how racial inequality is systematically perpetuated in a nation's institutions and social structures. Following Horkheimer's lead, African American sociologists Derrick Bell and Kimberlé Crenshaw further developed the CRT framework by arguing that racism is embedded in U.S. laws, institutions, and social structures. One critic has harshly defined CRT as "Black-supremacist racism, false history, and the terrible apotheosis of wokeness."[9]

---

8. Neal Hardin, "What Is Critical Race Theory," *Alliance Defending Freedom*, October 4, 2021, adflegal.org/article/what-critical-race-theory?sourcecode=10016058_r500&utm_source=grant&utm_medium=ppc&utm_campaign=Blog&gad_source=1&gclid=Cj0KCQjwq_G1BhCSARIsACc7Nxp9h-4kIUb-.

9. Jelani Cobb, "The Man Behind Critical Race Theory," *New Yorker*, September 13, 2021, www.newyorker.com/magazine/2021/09/20/the-man-behind-critical-race-theory.

Advocates of CRT have redefined racism, which, historically, has been understood as discrimination and prejudice based on race. Under CRT, however, racism is any disparity observed along racial lines. Racism, in this context, "is no longer regarded as a social attitude or philosophical belief, but is the objective expression of an inequality of power."[10] According to CRT theory, an individual, therefore, does not have to be prejudiced to participate in "racial oppression," but merely "occupy a 'privileged' position in an alleged hierarchy of groups and classes."[11] This redefinition shifts the emphasis from equality and equal treatment to equity and equal outcomes.[12] This shift is arguably "anti-American," as it paints America as structurally flawed and unjust, without any recognition given to the "American Dream" or the fact that diverse racial groups thrive in the West.

According to CRT, a singular villain often dominates the narrative—"white supremacy." Leftists and Islamists are obsessed with it, perceiving it in almost every sphere of Western life, viewing America and Israel as historically and inherently racist to their cores, and blaming "whiteness" and the white race's "domineering tendency" for most of the world's woes.[13] In the Israeli context, the same kind of warped ideology frames the Jewish state not as a legitimate democracy defending itself against authoritarian Islamist actors, but rather as the ultimate example of "settler-colonial whiteness" or "Zionist racism." Professors across the United States—and increasingly the broader West—integrate these kinds of rigid concepts into classroom discussions, which are then reinforced through peer pressure or the threat of academic repercussions if white students do not align with the Left's ideological orthodoxy.[14] For

10. Horowitz, *Unholy Alliance*, 151.

11. Ibid.

12. Hardin, "What Is Critical Race Theory," 2021.

13. Ibid.

14. Cameron Hilditch, "How Critical Race Theory Works," *National Review*,

some university students, the threat of "punishment" for failing to conform to these elements of CRT creates a "chilling effect" on freedom of speech. Even if students are not explicitly punished, they may self-censor to avoid social ostracization or potential career damage.

Far from creating a healthy environment for students, CRT's rejection of "colorblindness" and "meritocracy," which, arguably, represent ideal American principles, is detrimental to the well-being of students on university campuses, teaching them to view their peers through the lens of "oppression" and "racism," rather than as community members, fellow citizens, and potential friends.[15] It is no wonder, then, that CRT provides support to the Leftist-Islamist agenda, with its shared animosity toward Western values. Like CRT, Islamist theories view Western civilization as inherently corrupt, deeply unjust, and racist, without, of course, any introspection into the corruption, injustices, and racism within Muslim-majority countries. CRT and Islamism, at their roots, frame Muslims as the "victims" and that they, as such, should be ascribed a higher moral status, a dangerous and false assumption that strips Muslims of their own agency, individuality, and self-development. This alignment allows Islamists to suppress criticism of Islam and reinforce a climate of ideological conformity, with the Palestinian cause at its center.

CRT's integration into academic curricula appears to be at odds with public sentiment, with only 27 percent of Americans supporting its instruction in classrooms.[16] This public skepticism reflects an intuitive

---

May 8, 2021, www.nationalreview.com/2021/05/how-critical-race-theory-works/.

15. Emiliano Garcia-López and Enoch Sanchez, "Critical Race Theory," *Crossing the Divide*, n.d., crossing-the-divide.org/materials/critical-race-theory?gad_source=1&gclid=Cj0KCQjwq_G1BhCSARIsACc7Nxoy-iKua_KNo-towUr-1EDSY_amzq_4XEqiaOtiIB_ZE-ut4UxkbB0aAoJ0EALw_wcB.

16. The COVID States Project, "American Attitudes Toward Critical Race Theory," *Covid States*, October 2021, www.covidstates.org/reports/american-attitudes-toward-critical-race-theory.

understanding of CRT's divisive nature and its negative long-term effects, as it often reinforces schisms among students, cultivates an atmosphere where individuals are accused of "white supremacy," and consigns people to perpetual victimhood based on their racial identity. Such an approach offers no constructive path forward in the twenty-first century and beyond. Those responsible for designing academic curricula, including the bishops (professors who design their own syllabi), should shun these theories and prioritize civic principles, the "common ground," and a shared humanity among students.

SOCIAL JUSTICE: A NOBLE IDEA HIJACKED

CRT, to clarify, is not confined to academic theory. It has evolved into practical and DEI programs that now dominate university life. Indeed, numerous other sociological theories informed by critical theory, such as "critical social justice" or, more simply, "social justice," meaning the promotion of "a just society by challenging injustice and valuing diversity" so that "all people share a common humanity and therefore have a right to equitable treatment, support for their human rights, and a fair allocation of community resources."[17] Social justice sounds noble on the surface, but in its modern usage, it describes an ideology grounded in critical theory that advances a radical agenda rooted in racial politics.[18] This ideology prioritizes group identity and collective grievances over individual

---

17. Taylor & Francis, "What Is Social Justice? Definitions and Examples of Social Injustice," *Insights*, blog, n.d., insights.taylorandfrancis.com/social-justice/what-is-social-justice/#section-Contemporary-definitions-8qK0Um3dBz.
18. Jessica A. Kent, "What Is Social Justice Education and Why Does It Matter?" *Harvard Division of Continuing Education*, March 4, 2025, professional.dce.harvard.edu/blog/what-is-social-justice-education-and-why-does-it-matter/#What-is-Social-Justice-and-DEI-Education.

rights and freedom, risking social conflict and division.

In their pursuit of "equality" and "fairness," professors who center social justice ideology in their curricula have forged a new form of injustice, "reverse racism." Allan Johnson, the author of *Privilege, Power, and Difference*, captured the implicit racism in social justice curricula by arguing that white heterosexual males must make the "problem of [white] privilege" their own and "do something about it."[19] This mirrors the Marxist worldview, whereby white men, the "oppressors," are complicit in an oppressive system and thus true "liberation" for racial minorities will occur only when white people give up their rights in favor of the Leftists' classless utopia and the Islamists' global caliphate. Such requests clearly conflict with core Western values like individualism, meritocracy, and freedom. In its dissection of society, social justice ideology, ironically, often leaves us with more fractures than commonalities, raising the question of whether it is more "anti-social" than social.

Social justice ideology is also being coercively imposed through explicit curricular requirements and mandatory "diversity statements" for employment at Western universities. These statements are criticized for shifting focus from individual achievements to ideological conformity. Candidates are expected to submissively "bend the knee" and express loyalty to a specific set of ideas. As one academic put it, diversity statements are "clearly a form of compelled speech, and thus, a violation of First Amendment free speech protections."[20] By requiring candidates to articulate their commitment to specific identity groups and their experiences, we see a prioritization of group affiliations and their perceived experiences of "oppression." These ideological purity tests, enforced by

19. Allan G. Johnson, *Privilege, Power, and Difference* (New York: MacGraw-Hill, 2000), 10.

20. Zack K. De Piero, "The DEI Machine Has Always Been about Toeing an Ideological Line—Not Meaningful Change," *New York Post*, December 23, 2023, nypost.com/2023/12/23/opinion/dei-statements-are-bad-for-everyone/.

the bishops within the academy, are a subtle move on the chessboard to eliminate dissent before it can even enter the game.

Many institutions have explicit curricular requirements for social justice, often through course mandates, general education requirements, or diversity-focused learning outcomes. The University of California–Berkeley has an "American Cultures" requirement that focuses not on American culture, but on race, ethnicity, and indigeneity. At the same time, the University of Iowa requires incoming students to fulfill a "diversity and inclusion" curriculum requirement.[21] A parallel development is happening across Europe. At the European University Institute, all staff and researchers must complete mandatory online Equity, Diversity, and Inclusion (EDI) courses covering "foundational" concepts like "unconscious bias" and "harassment." Similarly, institutions such as Trinity College Dublin make EDI training compulsory for all staff serving on recruitment interview panels, while universities like the University of York require and monitor such training for promotion committees and leadership roles. This European embrace of mandatory EDI frameworks, though often justified in the name of "fairness" and "diversity," ultimately reveals an anti-Western orientation. By institutionalizing the presumption that "merit" is inherently tainted by systemic bias or "Eurocentrism," these requirements shift the university's mission away from truth and towards ideological enforcement.

The ascent of social justice ideology within academic institutions correlates with the rise of Diversity, Equity, and Inclusion (DEI) offices, which have been criticized for "punishing" professors who challenge their orthodoxy. An illustration of this phenomenon is the experience of Zack De Piero, a former professor at Penn State University, who contended in a *New York Post* article that his previous university's focus on

21. Jeff Charis-Carlson, "UI Sets New Diversity Requirement for 2017," *Iowa City Press-Citizen*, n.d., www.press-citizen.com/story/news/education/university-of-iowa/2015/12/21/ui-sets-new-diversity-requirement-2017/77694850/.

DEI cultivated "a hostile work environment teeming with discrimination," including being subjected to a video titled "White Teachers Are a Problem."[22] Following his public opposition to DEI, De Piero faced retaliation, as his "insubordination" was reported to the university's Affirmative Action Office. He was then sanctioned by both the university's human resources department and penalized in his annual performance review, a striking reminder of Orwell's insight, as he warned future generations of the dangers of measures demanding ideological conformity, which amounts to expressing fealty to an overlord, monarch, or authoritarian government.

The dominance of social justice in curricula has effectively turned college classrooms into "ground zero" for this threat, as noted by Maximilian Werner, a writing and rhetoric studies professor. He observed that "truth seeking and critical thinking" are now "subordinated to the ideology of critical social justice."[23] Werner criticized students for their "self-righteous, quasi-religious zeal," leading to classroom environments marked by unyielding dogma rather than critical thought. Werner contended that the ideas embraced by social justice and the assumptions behind it are so prevalent that they do not need explanation. This environment, where dissenting voices are marginalized or silenced, mirrors the tactics of authoritarian regimes, as Orwell described in *Nineteen Eighty-Four*, to enforce ideological conformity and suppress dissent.

While these developments within academic culture have become standard practice, a tide might be turning. In recent years, institutions

---

22. De Piero, "The DEI Machine Has Always Been about Toeing an Ideological Line—Not Meaningful Change"

23. Maximillian Werner, "Ground Zero—Critical Social Justice and Its Discontents," *Inside Higher Ed*, April 5, 2022, www.insidehighered.com/advice/2022/04/06/overzealous-social-justice-activists-can-curb-classroom-learning-opinion.

like the University of North Carolina[24] and the University of Massachusetts–Boston[25] have "un-required" mandatory diversity statements for student admission, employee recruitment, and faculty promotion. Many universities have subsequently phased out mandatory DEI statements following President Donald Trump's series of executive orders targeting diversity, equity, and inclusion programs in public and private universities.[26] Commending the Trump administration's dismantling of DEI, Representative Tim Walberg, a Republican from Michigan, issued the following statement that captured the views of Westerners unhappy with the rise and influence of social justice:

> For too long, social justice warriors crusaded to mandate DEI in every corner of America. Instead of merit, skills, and ability, DEI devotees pushed policies that are antithetical to American exceptionalism. From the classroom to the board room, Americans have felt the negative effects. DEI has bloated education budgets while telling students what to think instead of how to think.[27]

Much like an authoritarian system, the social justice movement suppresses dissent and demands ideological conformity. So, what can be

---

24. John D. Sailer, "A Death Knell for Diversity Statements," *City Journal*, March 25, 2025, www.city-journal.org/article/a-death-knell-for-diversity-statements.
25. Haley Gluhanich, "VICTORY—Umass Boston Quietly Removes DEI Requirements from Faculty Applications," FIRE, November 30, 2023, www.thefire.org/news/victory-umass-boston-quietly-removes-dei-requirements-faculty-applications.
26. The Leadership Conference on Civil and Human Rights, "Trump's Executive Orders on Diversity, Equity, and Inclusion, Explained," February 12, 2025, civilrights.org/resource/anti-deia-eos/.
27. Committee on Education and the Workforce, "Chairman Walberg on Trump's DEI Executive Orders," January 22, 2025, edworkforce.house.gov/news/documentsingle.aspx?DocumentID=412159.

done about this? One approach is to push back on group-based identity politics and promote viewpoint diversity and free speech in classrooms and on campuses. Creating an open marketplace of ideas would allow critical thought to flourish, rather than subordinating students to a single ideology. A second approach is to restore academic freedom, a foundational principle of the West's civic culture, by protecting professors who challenge social justice orthodoxy.

THE WAR OF POSITION: GRAMSCI'S BLUEPRINT FOR CULTURAL SUBVERSION

As I suggested in the Introduction, the weapons used in the "soft war" by the Leftist-Islamist alliance are not the traditional bombs and bullets, but rather ideologies and subversion. The current "non-violent" siege being waged by the alliance is undoubtedly influenced by Marxism, which was furthered more than eight decades ago by Antonio Gramsci.[28] Gramsci, an Italian communist, argued that challenging the established order required a "war of position"—a gradual subversion of cultural norms, values, and existing institutions to gain influence.[29] While this term originated with European military strategy theorists like Carl von Clausewitz, the Prussian general, and Antoine-Henri Jomini, the Swiss-French general, Gramsci appropriated it to develop his concept of hegemony in a cultural and political context. The goal of the "war of position," as one writer put it, is "to shape a new collective will of the masses" by infiltrating civil institutions "to weaken the defenses that civil

28. Bradley Thomas, "Antonio Gramsci—The Godfather of Cultural Marxism," *Foundation for Economic Education*, n.d., fee.org/articles/antonio-gramsci-the-godfather-of-cultural-marxism/.

29. Gonzalez and Gorka, "How Cultural Marxism Threatens the United States—and How Americans Can Fight It."

society provides to the current capitalist state."[30] This Gramscian "long march through the institutions" is how the Leftist-Islamist alliance subverts Western culture.

Gramsci's key concept is hegemony, the means by which a dominant group maintains power by shaping cultural beliefs and norms. He called for a counter-hegemony to be built within civil society, led by an intellectual leadership of its own, so that revolutionaries could then seize state power and establish a communist system. This resonates with both Leftists, who challenge "oppressive" cultural norms, and Islamists, who use "political Islam" as a revolutionary ideology.[31] These trends fly in the face of the American ideal of the "melting pot," where diverse cultures assimilate into a shared national consciousness. Instead, these groups rely on other metaphors, such as the increasingly popular "tossed salad" metaphor, in which a plethora of cultures retain their identities without fully blending (or assimilating). This vision for the United States undermines social cohesion by encouraging parallel societies rather than a more unified national identity. In effect, it would lead to the Balkanization of American society, in which groups, neighborhoods, and even regions would remain forever fragmented, and national bonds would be weakened.

The Balkanization process is already unfolding in Europe, as multiple scholarly and official assessments have documented in detail. The Migration Research Institute in Budapest, affiliated with the prestigious Mathias Corvinus Collegium, estimates roughly 900 uncontrolled "no-go zones" for non-Muslims throughout the continent.[32] In France

30. Thomas, "Antonio Gramsci—The Godfather of Cultural Marxism," n.d.

31. Juraj Butko, "Revelation or Revolution—A Gramscian Approach to the Rise of Political Islam," *British Journal of Middle Eastern Studies* 31 no. 1 (2004): 141–162.

32. Giulio Meotti, "Europe Is Turning Into One Big No-Go Zone," *Middle East Forum*, November 22, 2024, www.meforum.org/mef-online/europe-is-

alone, the Direction Générale de la Sécurité Intérieure (DGSI) has internally mapped 150 districts now effectively "in possession" of Islamist networks—enclaves, neighborhoods, and urban pockets—where French law has been replaced by parallel Islamist authority.[33] According to Alain Chouet, former deputy director of the French foreign intelligence service (DGSE), these Islamist districts now span 859 French cities and are home to approximately 4 million people—roughly 6 percent of France's total population.[34]

Gramscian theory offers a lens to understanding the dynamics of power within academic institutions, influencing both their overarching structures and the daily interactions on campus and in classrooms. In line with Gramsci, Leftists and Islamists argue that university norms are not "natural" occurrences, but rather constructed products of dominant "white" and "imperialist" ideologies. Students often embody Gramscian principles in their efforts to build counter-hegemony and counter-narratives. A recent experience in one of my own courses illustrates this dynamic clearly. A second-generation East African student who wears the hijab openly complained during class that the course content was "too Western" and failed to integrate "alternative theories" originating from Islamic and Third World perspectives. I sensed her intervention appeared designed to portray the curriculum—and by extension me—as inherently Western-centric, as if this were problematic, and potentially Islamophobic, thereby rallying students against the course content and the person teaching it. Both of these motives involve students creating and disseminating "alternative" viewpoints and understandings of issues, or, as some like me would consider it, anti-Western propaganda.

At Rice University, a Gramscian dynamic unfolded during the Black Lives Matter (BLM) movement. Students successfully campaigned to

---

turning-into-one-big-no-go-zone.

33. Ibid.

34. Ibid.

dismantle the "Willy Statue" of the university's founder, William Marshall Rice, which was deemed racist due to his ownership of slaves.[35] This was a "war of position" that led to a "war of maneuver" and a small but symbolic victory for the Leftist-Islamist alliance. Consequently, the main quad where the statue once stood was redesigned, and the statue itself was repositioned to a less prominent location, tucked into one of the quad's four corners. A platform that once held the statue, inscribed with American values like *E Pluribus Unum*, the Latin term meaning "Out of many, one," was also removed. This phrase, also the official motto of America, was apparently disregarded as irrelevant in the redesign.

Gramsci provided a framework for understanding how power operates not merely through political entities or brute force, as in traditional warfare, but through the control of culture and civil society. The professors who teach in Western academic institutions are the "bishops" who, in Gramsci's terms, are fighting a "war of position" from within society's trenches, where some professors are subtly moving their pieces to subvert the established order. Gramsci's strategy to subvert cultural norms resonates with Leftists and Islamists seeking to reshape Western civilization in their own image. Unbeknownst to them, Marx and Gramsci laid the groundwork for post-colonialism, a theory popularized by Frantz Fanon and later by Edward Said. I turn to these two theorists next.

POST-COLONIALISM: THE HARLOT OF HEGEMONY

While Gramsci provided the blueprint for cultural subversion, Frantz Fanon, a psychiatrist and philosopher whose experiences in French-colonized Algeria fueled his seminal works, *Black Skin, White Masks* and *The*

35. Stephen Simpson, "Rice University Relocates Its Founder's Remains after Reckoning with His Ties to Slavery," *Texas Tribune*, November 30, 2023, www.texastribune.org/2023/11/30/rice-university-founder-statue-remains/.

Wretched of the Earth, supplied the emotional and narrative ammunition that would later be aimed directly at the West and Israel. He is known primarily for his work on post-colonialism, an academic field concerned with the critical analysis of the ideological impact of Western colonization and its continuing influence, sometimes referred to in the academic literature as "neocolonialism." His two books noted above delved into the psychological scars of colonialism and how the colonizer—the "oppressor"—and the colonized—the "oppressed"—were trapped in a Manichaean dialectic of oppression and resistance. In them, he developed the term "internalized racism" to explore how the colonized can adopt the racist views of their colonizers, thus perpetuating their own "oppression." He was also critical of "interracial relationships," which he viewed as a form of "self-destruction," in that individuals desiring to "be white" did so to elevate their social, political, and cultural status by demonstrating more whiteness.[36]

Fanon's main assertion was the necessity of a violent struggle for true "liberation" as a means of "self-discovery" for the colonized. This sentiment laid the groundwork for a worldview that conflated Western power with inherent racism and oppression. His celebration of violence for the "colonized" echoes today in the U.S. and European contexts. In the United States, as we saw in the previous chapter, student groups invoke Fanonian "logic" to justify disruptive protests and the disruption of Jewish students as necessary "decolonizing" strategies. In Europe, Fanon-inspired narratives frame mass migration and the creation of parallel societies ("no-go zones") as a form of "resistance" against lingering "imperial" structures.

Recalling my earlier reflection on SJP's response to the *October 8* screening at Rice, I noted that the group's Instagram post decried my decision to screen the film. Fanon's influence is apparent in its phrasing,

---

36. John Drabinski, "Frantz Fanon," *Stanford Encyclopedia*, March 14, 2019, plato.stanford.edu/entries/frantz-fanon/.

which drew on decolonization theory and the psychology of oppression by stating that I was against "anti-imperialist perspectives" and that I had little concern for "communities already subjected to violence and erasure."[37] The post also claimed that Israel is an apartheid state, which is questionable given that diverse citizens have legal rights equal to Jewish citizens and enjoy more rights than the citizens of any Arab country in the Middle East.[38] It also painted Israel as a "colonial power," which ignores millennia-old Jewish links to the Holy Land. Jewish people have maintained a presence in the Holy Land over three millennia despite invasions by the Babylonians and Romans, and later by Arab Muslims, Christian Crusaders, Ottomans, and Europeans.

Post-colonial discourse often ignores other historical facts and forms of colonization, such as the Ottoman conquest of Constantinople in 1453. In that year, Muslim Turks, under the rule of Mehmet II, transformed the city into the seat of the Ottoman Empire. Constantinople, which the Ottomans renamed Istanbul, had served as a major center of Christendom for more than a thousand years. In the spirit of "decolonization," should Muslim Turks return the city to Greek Christians? Similarly, should the current Turkish state withdraw its troops from northern Cyprus, a territory it has occupied since 1974 as a protector of the island's minority Turkish Cypriot population, which itself arrived only in 1571 following the Ottoman conquest of the Greek-majority island? While these questions are rhetorical, they highlight a critique of decolonization studies: it centers "non-white" frameworks, thereby creating an inconsistent standard for judging colonial legacies.

This historical perspective leads to a complicated predicament.

---

37. Rice University Students for Justice in Palestine, "Tuesday's Screening of the Film October 8 at Rice University," 2025.

38. Mark Dubowitz, "Israel Must Reclaim Its Arab Citizens," *Jerusalem Post*, November 18, 2022, www.fdd.org/analysis/op_eds/2022/11/18/israel-must-reclaim-its-arab-citizens/.

Which group has never been colonized, and which groups have never been the colonizers? I raise this issue not to diminish the pain that colonization has inflicted upon people throughout the centuries, but to consider historical facts. Fanon supporters within academia selectively employ anti-colonial theory as a means to ignite a revolution, with the ultimate goal of subverting Western culture and transforming nations like the United States into socialist and communist worlds. This would entail the destruction of long-standing civic values and democratic systems that Western powers have enjoyed and defended for centuries, systems that have undoubtedly served them—and the world—well.

ORIENTALISM: SAID'S LEGACY, OCCIDENTALISM, AND THE BATTLE OF NARRATIVES

As Fanon's post-colonial thought further solidified the critique of Western culture in the 1960s, another significant voice—Edward Said—emerged. His concept of "Orientalism" refined Gramsci's analysis of cultural hegemony by positing that the West, through colonization during the eighteenth to twentieth centuries, deliberately constructed a backward, exotic, and inferior representation of the East (the Orient) to justify Western expansion. A professor of literature at Columbia University, Said framed his concept in terms of a binary—the West as civilized, rational, and superior—versus the East as uncivilized, irrational, and inferior. His book *Orientalism: Western Conceptions of the Orient* even begins with a quote from Marx—"They cannot represent themselves; they must be represented"—highlighting a shared belief that marginalized groups lack agency and representation.

Critics of Said argued that he focused solely on the "Orientalist" framework from the West, ignoring the reciprocal and equally reductive "Occidentalist" views from the East. Returning to the Ottoman Empire, there were periods of its reign where Muslims functioned as colonizers, and parts of the West were stereotyped to justify its colonization. Ottoman narratives often depicted European Christians as "infidels," "barbarians," or "technologically inferior."[39] While not always leading to direct colonization in the same manner as European expansion, the Ottoman conquest and long-term rule over European territories and Christians in Bulgaria, Greece, Hungary, and Serbia involved Occidental frameworks. You rarely, however, hear about these moments in history in university classrooms, as they do not align with the dominant narrative—that the West, White people, Americans, and now Israelis are the true perpetrators of colonization and imperialism.

Just as the Ottoman Empire constructed its own Occidental narratives to rationalize its centuries-long dominion over much of Eastern Europe, so too can individuals encounter reductive portrayals of their own culture. I recall my experiences as a master's student at Royal Holloway, University of London, in the winter of 2007, when I had an encounter that illuminated the dynamics of such "cultural essentialism." One of my English peers, critical of President George W. Bush's "War on Terror" in Afghanistan and Iraq, engaged me in a discussion. While I shared some of his criticism of those wars, this marked my first experience of overt anti-Americanism while abroad. The exchange quickly soured, devolving into generalized stereotypes of Americans as "ignorant," "insular," and "violent." I felt mischaracterized, reduced to a caricature rather than recognized as an individual. In subsequent years, this phenomenon continued to manifest, with my social media interactions frequently descending into Occidental viewpoints, with Islamists labeling me an "infidel" and disparaging me as an American "terrorist." Whether Orientalist or Occidental, these kinds of reductive perspectives fuel the anti-Western agenda at the heart of the Leftist-Islamist alliance.

---

39. Arda Eksigil, "Ottoman Visions of the West (15th–17th Centuries), *McGill University*, December 2014, escholarship.mcgill.ca/downloads/cr56n4060.

For college students and activist groups like SJP, acknowledging that the Orient also constructed—and currently constructs—stereotypical images of the "West" would certainly challenge their Marxist worldview. Occidentalism challenges the "oppressed" versus "oppressor" binary by moving beyond a singular focus on Western culpability. Orientalism, by contrast, allows radical students to dismiss all Western narratives concerning regions like the Middle East as inherently "biased" or "propagandistic."

The theories posited by Marx, Gramsci, Fanon, and Said—carefully taught and amplified by the bishops in university departments— open up a complex terrain where denouncing and rejecting the West takes precedence over critical examination of "non-Western" forms of oppression, of which there are many around the world, particularly concerning the current state of Christians in Muslim-majority countries worldwide.[40]

WEAPONIZING ISLAMOPHOBIA: HOW ACADEMICS SILENCE DISSENT AND FUEL THE LEFTIST-ISLAMIST ALLIANCE

The term "Islamophobia" became popular during my doctoral studies at Trinity College Dublin, a period between 2010 and 2014, when my research focused on Islamic studies, Christian and Muslim relations, and the relationship between the West and Islam. It was introduced and defined in the 1997 Runnymede Trust report titled *Islamophobia: A Challenge for Us All*, written by a collective of British academics who sought to define the dynamics of anti-Islamic sentiment. The report established a framework based on the Manichaean binary of "closed views" and "open views" of Islam.[41] Closed views were characterized by perceiving Islam

40. I have addressed this subject—alongside Islamophobia—in my previous eight books.

41. Runnymede Trust, "Islamophobia—A Challenge for Us All," Runnymede

as monolithic, separate, inferior, an enemy, manipulative, and discriminatory. Conversely, "open views" embraced Islam as diverse, interactive, unique, a partner, and sincere. This initial framing, while benign, laid the groundwork for the binary that would later be weaponized by the Leftist-Islamist alliance to dismiss any criticism of Islam as "bigoted" or "racist."

Islamist organizations in the United Kingdom, most notably Hizb ut-Tahrir—which openly advocates for a global caliphate and rejects Enlightenment principles—routinely accuse critics of "Islamophobia" to silence legitimate discussion of Islamist ideology and terrorist groups such as Hamas and Hezbollah. British authorities have recognized this tactic. Sara Khan, the United Kingdom's former Lead Commissioner for Countering Extremism, stated, "[Hizb ut-Tahrir] and their sympathizers weaponize Islamophobia in an attempt to shut down legitimate debate about Islamic extremism while undermining the general struggle against anti-Muslim hatred."[42] The same pattern appears in the American context with groups such as the Council on American-Islamic Relations (CAIR), which I have experienced directly. After I publicly criticized the pro-Hamas student protests sweeping U.S. campuses in 2024 via social media, CAIR leaders lumped me into the "Islamophobic" crowd, as did graduate students in my own department, who issued a collective letter accusing me of using "Islamophobic dog whistles"—apparently for the simple act of denouncing terrorism and those "foot soldiers" who support it. That is how low the bar has fallen—merely condemning terrorist groups and their sympathizers is now treated as evidence of anti-Mus-

---

Trust, 1997, www.runnymedetrust.org/publications/islamophobia-a-challenge-for-us-all.

42. Sara Khan, quoted in Camilla Turner, "Hard Line Groups Are 'Weaponising' Islamophobia, Government's Counter-Extremism Tsar Warns," *Telegraph*, September 15, 2018. www.telegraph.co.uk/education/2018/09/15/hard-line-groups-weaponising-islamophobia-governments-counter/.

lim bigotry. We have reached a point where distinguishing between legitimate criticism of Islamist ideology and genuine prejudice against Muslims has become deliberately blurred. "Blurring" is a key strategy of the Leftist-Islamist alliance, which exploits the West's tolerance and legal protections for freedom of religion by inverting them. This strategy transforms rational criticism—a cornerstone of Enlightenment values—into accusations of racism and discrimination. It is all, to be clear, Orwellian—language is systematically twisted so that criticism becomes "hate" and defense of Western values becomes "oppression."

The pre–mass-media era in which the Runnymede Trust report was published meant that its impact was confined to academic and policymaking circles. However, with the explosion of the blogosphere, social media, and other media platforms, a new phenomenon emerged—the "Islamophobia industry." Nathan Lean, a professor at North Carolina State University, documented this phenomenon in his book *The Islamophobia Industry: How the Right Manufactures Fear of Muslims*, which explored the network of intellectuals, organizations, philanthropists, and political entities whose criticisms of Islam were perceived by many as promoting anti-Muslim violence.[43] My second book, *Muslims in America: Examining the Facts*, addressed many of the issues Lean highlighted, leading me to seek his endorsement, which appeared on the book's back cover.[44] Our relationship, however, began to unravel in 2020, coinciding with what I refer to as my own "awakening." While I embraced the liberating spirit of the Abraham Accords and the promise of deeper Jewish, Christian, and Muslim relations, Lean clung to the victimhood narrative, seeing Muslims, and especially Palestinians, as the perpetu-

43. Nathan Lean, *The Islamophobia Industry: How the Right Manufactures Fear of Muslims* (London: Pluto Press, 2012).
44. Craig Considine, *Muslims in America: Examining the Facts* (New York: Bloomsbury, 2018).

ally "oppressed" group,[45] while at the same time turning a blind eye to Hamas's repressive governing tactics. This reflects a questionable tactic frequently employed by the likes of Lean—they conflate any denunciation of Hamas, its violent antisemitic ideology, or the broader pattern of Palestinian-inspired terrorism with "Islamophobic." In their inverted moral framework, criticizing jihadist groups or refusing to excuse rocket attacks against Israeli civilians is reframed as hatred of Islam or Muslims themselves.

Our ideological divergence hit a zenith after October 7, 2023, when I became more vocal in defending Israel. Lean publicly attacked me on X in May 2024, amidst the height of the SJP-led encampments on college campuses, after I posted on X an image of a Marxist flyer spotted in New York City, which included calls like "Death to America" and "Death to Israel." Lean deemed the flyer "troubling" and not representative of the SJP-led protests more broadly. He branded my X post "disgusting and abusive," adding, "You've been a snake all along, lying quietly in wait."[46] A few months later, he escalated his attacks, claiming that I had either "astonishingly abandoned" my moral integrity or that I never possessed any to begin with.[47] His response mirrors Orwell's warning that Leftists demonize dissent, a revelation of the intolerance underlying the Leftist-Islamist alliance, where intellectual freedom "bends the knee" to conformity and ideological purity.

Lean's fury over my shift was so intense that he even contacted Bloomsbury Publishing, the publisher of my book, demanding they re-

---

45. Nathan Lean, "Notice the relative clarity of this headline from the New York Times—its main clause in active voice . . .," X, post dated May 15, 2025, x.com/nathanlean/status/1923119107462832404.

46. Nathan Lean, X, post dated May 3, 2024, x.com/nathanlean/status/1786468387268477381.

47. Nathan Lean, X, post dated July 29, 2024, x.com/nathanlean/status/1817903503525687662.

move his endorsement from the back cover.[48] One might wryly observe that such attempts at intellectual erasure are typically the domain of communist countries or Islamist regimes, not Western academics or supposed champions of academic freedom. His reaction exemplifies how, in certain academic circles, any deviation from the established narrative of "Muslim victimhood" and "Palestinian oppression," or any critique of Islamist ideology, is labeled as "Islamophobia" or a "betrayal." This tactic, championed by the "bishops," ensures that anything considered critical or harsh toward Muslims or Islam is silenced, serving as a powerful tool for the Leftist-Islamist alliance to control the narrative and enforce ideological purity.

Beyond silencing dissent and penalizing independent thought, the term "Islamophobia" has been strategically weaponized as a tool to advance an Islamist agenda, one readily co-opted by Leftist groups. The Leftist-Islamist alliance deploys "Islamophobia" as a political construct, not merely to protect "political Islam" from scrutiny or opposition, but to gain leverage within civil society and the public sphere. A salient example of this is the Council on American-Islamic Relations (CAIR), a group claiming to be a civil rights organization, which alleges that government counterterrorism programs, like the Targeted Violence and Terrorism Prevention (TVTP) program, are inherently "Islamophobic," arguing they disproportionately target Muslim communities and lead to discrimination and surveillance.[49] While legitimate concerns regarding

48. Nathan Lean, "May others join them in solidarity. My email to Bloomsbury, below," X, post dated May 2, 2024, x.com/nathanlean/status/1786037485031600158.

49. Council on American-Islamic Relations, "CAIR Joins 70+ Civil Rights Groups in Letter to DHS Opposing 'Countering Violent Extremism' (CVE) Program Based on Junk Science, Targeting Vulnerable Communities," Council on American-Islamic Relations, June 2, 2020, www.cair.com/press_releases/cair-joins-70-civil-rights-groups-in-letter-to-dhs-opposing-countering-violent-extremism-cve-program-based-on-junk-science-targeting-vulnerable-c-

civil liberties and potential discrimination are valid—and indeed, such practices would be Orwellian and antithetical to the principles that I espouse—groups like CAIR exploit the "Islamophobia" label to undermine vital security efforts by branding them as "bigoted" and "racist." This tactic of positioning counterextremism as an attack on the entire Muslim community is disingenuous and a dangerous misrepresentation of reality.

This issue is particularly critical given the problematic interpretations of Islamic scripture and practices that demonstrably lead to persecution, as evidenced by the widespread targeting of Christians in the Muslim world, who are frequently deemed "infidels" and subject to second-class citizenship. In extreme cases, such as in Nigeria[50] and Pakistan,[51] Christians face deadly assaults from groups like Boko Haram or are accused of blasphemy—effectively committing Orwellian "thought-crimes"—for merely speaking about Muhammad, the main prophet of Islam. Any rational observer would be alarmed by such deadly extremism and the stark absence of free speech in Muslim societies around the world.

My point is that Westerners, especially academics devoted to the pursuit of truth and genuine knowledge, should be granted the ability to critique elements of Islam, especially its radical elements, without the automatic accusation of "Islamophobia." This suppression of critical thought contributes to Gramsci's "war of position" to control discourse in civil society. These kinds of ideological conformity, enforced through the lexicon of sociological theories analyzed throughout this chapter, are

---

ommunities/.

50. Open Doors USA, "Nigeria—World Watch Ranking," Open Doors USA, 2025, www.opendoors.org/en-US/persecution/countries/nigeria/.

51. Open Doors USA, "Pakistan—World Watch Ranking," Open Doors USA, 2025, www.opendoors.org/en-US/persecution/countries/pakistan/.

systematically mainstreaming "cultural Marxism" in scholarly communities and in the minds of college students across the country.

HUNTINGTON RECONSIDERED: NAVIGATING THE CLASH WITHIN AND FOSTERING INTERFAITH SYNTHESIS

After many years writing about the importance of interfaith dialogue, I have come to realize that the most pressing conflict today is within, not necessarily between, civilizations. My journey toward this realization began in 2004 as an undergraduate student at American University in Washington, D.C., in a class taught by Akbar Ahmed, a former Pakistani ambassador to the United Kingdom, who offered an understanding of jihad as a spiritual struggle, not a "holy war," echoing Muhammad's teaching that the greater jihad is not one of "bombs" and "bullets," but rather one of "introspection" and "reflection." Throughout my time in the course, Ahmed championed nonviolence, interfaith dialogue, people-to-people diplomacy, and the power of knowledge in bridging cultural and religious divides. His message of unity struck me as a far superior path to peace than the prevailing narratives of conflict and war, which dominated most of my other undergraduate courses at American University.

Early in the course, Ahmed rejected Samuel Huntington's "Clash of Civilizations" thesis, which predicted that, following the dissolution of the Soviet Union and the triumph of Western democracies and capitalism, the next major global conflict would be drawn along religious or cultural lines—namely, between the Western world and one or more competing civilizations, with the Islamic world identified as a primary challenger.[52] As a committed advocate for dialogue and peace, Ahmed

52. Samuel P. Huntington, "The Clash of Civilizations?" *Foreign Affairs* 72 no. 3 (Summer 1993): 22–49.

criticized the crude binary of "the West versus Islam" because it overlooked centuries of cultural and religious exchange, as well as historical periods where Occidental Christians and Oriental Muslims not only coexisted but also thrived together. Ahmed's commitment to building bridges meant he refused to accept conflict as an inevitable fate, believing instead in a world where Christians and Muslims could find common ground and foster positive relationships.

The events of 9/11, however, seemed to validate Huntington's prediction. Muslim extremists conducted the attacks, and the U.S. government, backed by many of its Western allies, responded by invading Afghanistan and Iraq. Osama bin Laden, the terrorist mastermind of the 9/11 attacks, used the Marxist binary of "oppressed" versus "oppressor" by positioning the Muslim world as the former and decrying Western culture as the epitome of sinfulness and evil. The situation was further compounded when U.S. president George W. Bush suggested that America's fight was akin to a "new Crusade."[53] This framing evoked the historical memory of the four-hundred-year period in the Middle Ages when Christian and Muslim armies clashed over land, resources, and perceived divine supremacy.

At that stage of my life, influenced by these events and my idealism rooted in interfaith dialogue and peacemaking, I, too, rejected Huntington's thesis. For years, I criticized his theory, proclaiming him "wrong" for simplifying Western and Islamic civilization into monoliths, overlooking historical periods of harmony between the West and Islam, and ignoring contemporary examples of Westerners and Muslims sharing similar global visions for society and the future. Today, my understanding of Huntington's theory has evolved, becoming far more nuanced.

---

53. Neil Johnston and Fiona Parker, "George Bush Saw Iraq War as Part of Biblical Crusade Against 'Evil Doers,'" *Telegraph*, July 22, 2025, www.telegraph.co.uk/news/2025/07/22/george-bush-iraq-war-biblical-crusade-against-evil-doers/.

While I still do not fully embrace his binary positioning of the West versus Islam, my current perspective acknowledges certain realities. It is intellectually dishonest for me to deny that elements within Islamic civilization, such as Hamas and Iran, categorically reject Western values and the West's role in the world. Similarly, within Western nations, there are those who view Islam in monolithic terms, perceiving it as the ultimate enemy of Western civilization. For Westerners, it is crucial to recognize and empower those elements within the Muslim world who actively seek to collaborate with the West for a better future.

In my book *Beyond Dialogue: Building Bonds Between Christians and Muslims*, I utilized Huntington's Clash of Civilizations theory as part of a tripartite framework.[54] This framework explored the Dialogue of Civilizations and, critically, the Synthesis of Civilizations, which served as my main contribution to the body of knowledge on the relationship between the West and Islam. The Dialogue of Civilizations, championed by figures such as Pope Francis and former Iranian president Mohammad Khatami, advocates for dialogue, cross-cultural communication, and religious literacy. While I embraced all these elements in *Beyond Dialogue*, my argument was that mere dialogue and people-to-people diplomacy are insufficient for genuinely addressing the challenges posed by diversity. Throughout the book, I urged readers to transcend superficial tolerance and move beyond dialogue to a deeper "synthesis." This synthesis involves uniting around shared goals and values and actively collaborating in the public sphere to demonstrate the fruits of their cooperation and friendship.

A living embodiment of the Synthesis of Civilizations is the United Arab Emirates' Abrahamic Family House initiative. This interfaith structure, which includes a synagogue, church, and mosque alongside each other, stands as a physical testament to the possibility of unity

54. Craig Considine, *Beyond Dialogue—Building Bonds Between Christians and Muslims* (London: Polity, 2025).

among Jews, Christians, and Muslims, and by extension, between the West and Islam. While it is just a single structure in one part of the Muslim world, dismissing it as a "one-off" or "irrelevant" project would be a significant oversight and a strategic error in the war between the Leftist-Islamist alliance and the West. As the recent U.S.-Israel–led war against Iran demonstrates, the Emiratis are key allies of the Americans and Israelis, and they strive to build a Middle East based on cooperation and friendship instead of conflict and friction. When Westerners broadly identify Islam as the root of all evil, it marginalizes these crucial voices who advocate for a vision of the world vastly different from that promoted by Islamist groups. Such dismissal would, in fact, create an obstacle to interfaith dialogue and peacebuilding—which the Leftist-Islamist alliance rejects due to their shared destructive approaches to "resolving" complex twenty-first-century conflicts.

THE THEORETICAL BATTLEFIELD: FROM ACADEMIC SUBVERSION TO CIVIL SOCIETY

The theories examined in this chapter—cultural Marxism, CRT, social justice ideology, Gramsci's cultural hegemony and war of position, Fanon's celebration of violence, and Said's Orientalism—supply the intellectual ammunition for the pawns on the front lines. To fully grasp the Leftist-Islamist alliance's power, we must now turn our attention to the civil sphere and to the alliance's key organizations and networks that are working to remake the West in their own image.

Chapter 3

THE ARCHITECTURE OF THE LEFTIST-ISLAMIST ALLIANCE: ORGANIZATIONS AND NETWORKS

To understand how the Leftist-Islamist alliance sustains its "soft war," we must examine the organizations and networks that serve as its "knights" on the chessboard. Operating in the civil sphere rather than on traditional battlefields, these groups provide the funding, training, legal cover, and ideological coordination that turn campus pawns into an effective fighting force. Channeling the defining principle of Sun Tzu's *The Art of War*—that "all warfare is based on deception"—the knights present themselves as civil rights or humanitarian organizations while advancing a coordinated campaign against the U.S.-Israel alliance and the West at large. This chapter maps the architecture of these alliances, beginning with the group that most directly orchestrates SJP activism on American college campuses.

CALLING THE TUNE: AMERICAN MUSLIMS FOR PALESTINE (AMP) AND THE ORCHESTRATION OF SJP ACTIVISM

My experiences with groups like SJP have taught me to question the "behind-the-scenes" forces that orchestrate their operations in the public realm. This has led me to an important question regarding SJP's influence: who truly sets their agenda? The enduring proverb, "He who pays the piper calls the tune," is an appropriate frame of reference. This phrase, which first appeared in print in English jurist John Selden's posthumously published book *Table-Talk*, sheds light on how musicians (like a piper or violinist) in medieval and early modern Europe were hired for events like fairs, military marches, or weddings. Whoever hired the musician decided the music to be played because they were paying for the service. The proverb means that any person or entity providing money, resources, and support to a person, group, or organization has the right and power to dictate how things are done or what the outcome will be. In simple terms, whoever funds something has control over it.

In this case, American Muslims for Palestine (AMP) is the patron calling the tune for SJP. Founded in Chicago, Illinois, in 2006, AMP is a nonprofit corporation that facilitates activism on university campuses across the United States. It is described as a successor entity to the Holy Land Foundation for Relief and Development (HLF),[1] which had been hailed as the largest U.S. Muslim charity before its activities were terminated in 2001, when the U.S. Treasury Department designated it as a terrorist organization under Executive Order 13224. In 2008, five HLF leaders were convicted of financing terrorism for giving material support—approximately $12.4 million over a period of roughly six years—to Hamas.[2] Four former HLF employees now work for AMP, which

1. Canary Mission, "The Holy Land Five," June 2, 2025, canarymission.org/campaign/The_Holy_Land_Five.

2. Jonathan Schanzer, "From Ivory Towers to Dark Corners—Investigating the

frequently sponsors events featuring former HLF leaders and their families.[3] The continuity here is visible, ensuring that their Islamist ideology continues to be played, albeit by new pipers—university students and their affiliated organizations. In fact, on April 15, 2026, Georgetown University's SJP chapter held a letter-writing event to "stand in solidarity with our comrades . . . caged by the U.S. empire for their resistance to occupation and repression."[4] SJP-Georgetown solicited letters of support for "political prisoners"—namely, the founders of the Holy Land Foundation, Ghassan Elashi and Shukri Abu Baker, along with criminals who torched New York Police Department cars and repeatedly attacked Jews.

AMP provides financial support to SJP and also trains its leaders in methods of activism, like procuring grants, materials, and speakers, and assisting them in printing materials. The organization operates with little financial transparency, as it receives tax-exempt donations through its fiscal sponsor, the nonprofit organization Americans for Justice in Palestine Educational Foundation (AJP), allowing AMP to maintain a façade of legal separation,[5] even though the AJP shares officers and a Chicago

---

Nexus Between Antisemitism, Tax-exempt Universities, and Terror Financing," House Ways and Means Committee, November 15, 2023, gop-waysandmeans.house.gov/wp-content/uploads/2023/11/Schanzer-Testimony.pdf.

3. James Comers, "Letter to National Students for Justice in Palestine," House of Representatives Committee on Oversight and Accountability, May 29, 2024, oversight.house.gov/wp-content/uploads/2024/05/Letter-to-National-SJP-5.29.24.pdf.

4. Jessica Costescu, "Georgetown SJP Solicits Letters of Support For 'Political Prisoners' Convicted of Funneling Millions To Hamas," *Washington Free Beacon*, April 24, 2026, freebeacon.com/campus/georgetown-sjp-solicits-letters-of-support-for-political-prisoners-convicted-of-funneling-millions-to-hamas/.

5. Jonathan Schanzer, "Israel Imperiled—Threats to the Jewish State," House of Representatives Foreign Affairs Committee, April 19, 2016, docs.house.gov/meetings/FA/FA18/20160419/104817/HHRG-114-FA18-Wstate-SchanzerJ-20160419.pdf

office with AMP.[6] The AJP claims to be a public benefit corporation that uses its revenue to publish books, fund research on international relations, and support conferences, but critics argue that it serves as one of Hamas's propaganda arms in the United States.[7] This organizational structure raises concerns about the true nature of AMP's activities and funding, particularly given its close relationship with SJP and the group's impact on campus cultures nationwide.

AMP's lack of transparency is a concern to congressional lawmakers in Washington, D.C. Republican Senator Bill Cassidy, the chair of the Senate Committee on Health, Education, Labor, and Pensions (HELP), opened an investigation into AMP for its connections to SJP.[8] HELP's investigation claimed that the group has helped organize, support, and facilitate violent, antisemitic demonstrations following October 7 and that at least nine individuals with ties to AMP and AJP have alleged past or present connections to Hamas.[9] In another case, in May 2024, Republican Representative James Comer from Kentucky—the chair of the Committee on Oversight and Accountability (CCOA) in the House of Representatives—sent a letter to Osama Abu Irshaid, the executive

---

6. Ibid.

7. Influence Watch, "Americans for Justice in Palestine Educational Foundation," *Influence Watch*, n.d., www.influencewatch.org/non-profit/americans-for-justice-in-palestine-educational-foundation/.

8. Michael Starr, "US Senate committee investigating AMP for alleged Hamas connections," *Jerusalem Post*, March 30, 2025, www.jpost.com/diaspora/antisemitism/article-848086.

9. U.S. Senate Committee on Health, Education, Labor, and Pensions, "Chair Cassidy Launches HELP Investigation into Organization with Alleged Ties to Hamas, Antisemitic Violence on College Campuses," U.S. Senate Committee on Health, Education, Labor, and Pensions, March 28, 2025, www.help.senate.gov/rep/newsroom/press/chair-cassidy-launches-help-investigation-into-organization-with-alleged-ties-to-hamas-antisemitic-violence-on-college-campuses.

director of AMP, regarding his organization's activities at U.S. universities.[10] Comer's letter mentioned *The Written Resistance*, an SJP publication, which was curiously launched in September 2023, mere days before October 7, and an April 2024 article in the same publication that positively cited Mao Zedong, the Chinese communist revolutionary (for more on Mao Zedong, see chapter 5).

Abu Irshaid has been a prominent figure at campus protests. On Columbia's campus in 2023, he declared, "This is not only a genocide that is being committed in Gaza. . . . This is also a war on us here in America," which to many signaled a call to intifada on the domestic front.[11] Two days later, he appeared at George Washington University in Washington, D.C., where he delivered another inflammatory speech:

> [The U.S. and Israel] know they are going against the force of history. They are trying to destroy you before you succeed in bringing this imperialism to an end, before we bring this poison of Zionism to an end. . . . Now, we know what America stands for. We know what these elite colleges stand for. They are only structures in an imperial project. Israel is only another structure of an imperial project. Zionism is no less evil than white supremacy or any sort of supremacy. . . . We will stand with our morality and we will maintain our future in terms of our professionalism and in terms of how we are going to change this country forever. They are lying to us about American exceptionalism. . . . Zionism will be a dark moment in our history. Any sort of supremacy will be a dark moment in our history. It is you, it is your generation, that will bring this to an end. It is you that will bring this

---

10. House of Representatives, "National Students for Justice in Palestine," Congress of the United States, May 29, 2024, 2, oversight.house.gov/wp-content/uploads/2024/05/Letter-to-National-SJP-5.29.24.pdf.

11. Will Carless and Romina Ruiz-Goiriena, "Amid campus protests, organizers with past ties to Hamas support also emerge," *USA Today*, May 22, 2024, www.usatoday.com/story/news/investigations/2024/05/22/gaza-student-protests-american-muslims-for-palestine/73775372007/.

disgrace to an end.[12]

It is safe to assume Abu Irshaid's target was not just the U.S.-Israel alliance but also the entirety of Western civilization. While he pointed to the "force of history"—a Marxist framework leaning towards a communist utopian vision—his rhetoric contained all the basic elements of the Leftist-Islamist agenda— opposition to "Western imperialism," condemnation of "white supremacy," and expression of anti-American rhetoric. His demeaning of academic institutions as "structures" within the "imperial project" draws on both Marxist and Gramscian ideologies to advocate the destruction of such "evil" societal institutions. Notably, his claim that Zionism is "poison" is considered antisemitic, as it denies the Jewish connection to their ancestral homeland.

Overall, Abu Irshaid's chilling call to students—i.e., the "foot soldiers" (pawns)—to pick up their figurative weapons to change America forever should alarm any academic or politician. Thankfully, federal agents seized his electronic devices upon his return to the United States from Qatar in June 2024 and interrogated him on his role in organizing protests following October 7.[13] He was previously placed on the U.S. government's "no-fly list" out of concern that he was a Hamas propagandist.[14]

---

12. Middle East Media Research Institute, "Executive Director of 'American Muslims For Palestine" Osama Abuirshaid At George Washington University Encampment—We Will Take Back America, Just Like We Will Take Back Palestine; You Will Be The Past, We Will Be The Future," *MEMRI*, April 25, 2024, www.memri.org/tv/executive-director-american-muslims-palestine-osama-abuirshaid-george-washington-university-encampment-change-america-zionism-removed.

13. Justia, "Abu Irshaid et al v. Garland et al," Justia, 2025, law.justia.com/cases/federal/district-courts/virginia/vaedce/1:2024cv01405/558412/30/.

14. Matthew Farrell, "Palestinian-American plaintiffs file suit against US Attorney General over placement on terrorism watchlist," *Jurist News*, Au-

The AMP-SJP entity is not explicitly active on European campuses and streets, but the continent has its own "knights," including the Samidoun Palestinian Prisoner Solidarity Network. Samidoun operates across the European Union, with particularly strong activity in Belgium, France, Greece, the Netherlands, Spain, and Sweden. Like SJP, it coordinates large pro-Palestinian protests and "Resistance Festivals" that frequently celebrate "armed resistance" by groups such as Hamas and the PFLP. Samidoun's Belgium-based European coordinator, Mohammed Khatib, has faced repeated legal pressure. Belgium revoked his refugee status in 2025 and cited him as a "radical hate preacher" who supports Hamas and the PFLP. He has also been arrested, subjected to entry bans, and detained, including in Greece in early 2026. Another group of "knights" is the Palestine Solidarity Campaign (PSC), which is based in the United Kingdom. Founded in 1982, the PSC is one of the longest-running and largest pro-Palestinian entities in Europe. It organizes major demonstrations, lobbies politicians, promotes BDS-style campaigns, and works closely with Leftist groups, among them trade unions and activist coalitions. Far from being isolated, this Western network of activists works to erode the moral and strategic legitimacy of the U.S.-Israel alliance. Even more significantly, it is laying siege to Western civilization from within, drawing on Gramsci's strategy of the "war of position" to gradually erode cultural norms.

The AMP's sphere of influence extends beyond SJP and university campuses. The group's lobbying arm—AJP Action—has actively engaged with "progressive" lawmakers in the House of Representatives, including Ilhan Omar, Rashida Tlaib, Andre Carson, Betty McCollum, Bill Pascrell, and Jan Schakowsky—all Democrats.[15] The AMP and AJP's ability

---

gust 13, 2024, www.jurist.org/news/2024/08/palestinian-american-plaintiffs-file-suit-against-us-attorney-general-over-placement-on-terrorism-watchlist/.

15. Schanzer, "From Ivory Towers to Dark Corners—Investigating the Nexus

to reach the halls of Congress demonstrates that it has the necessary strategic support to advance their revolutionary agenda across multiple fronts within American society (see chapter 4).

These groups are far from the only "knights" in this network. Other organizations play critical roles in funding, shielding, and legitimizing the Leftist-Islamist alliance's activities.

FROM ALLY TO ADVERSARY: MY JOURNEY WITH CAIR

While AMP and AJP coordinate much of the campus activism in the United States, the Council on American-Islamic Relations (CAIR) is the country's most influential Islamist organization. Along with the work of a number of academics, it provides the broader legal, political, and public-relations infrastructure for the alliance. I once viewed CAIR as "civil society actors," a testament to how easily one can be misled by carefully cultivated public images like CAIR's. The organization has been identified as a Muslim Brotherhood group by the U.S. Congress[16] and Texas Governor Greg Abbott,[17] and was listed as an "unindicted co-conspirator" in the HLF trial for supporting Hamas.[18] During the

---

Between Antisemitism, Tax-Exempt Universities, and Terror Financing," 2023.

16. U.S. House of Representatives, "H.R. 4097, Designate CAIR as a Terrorist Organization Act," 119th Cong., 1st sess., June 24, 2025, www.congress.gov/bill/119th-congress/house-bill/4097/text.

17. Office of the Governor, "A Proclamation Designating the Muslim Brotherhood and CAIR as Foreign Terrorist and Transnational Criminal Organizations under the Texas Law," November 18, 2025, gov.texas.gov/uploads/files/press/PROC_declaring_Muslim_Brotherhood_and_CAIR_Transnational_Criminal_Organizations_IMAGE_11-18-2025.pdf.

18. U.S. Department of Justice, "Review of FBI Interactions with the Council on American-Islamic Relations," U.S. Department of Justice, September 2013, oig.justice.gov/reports/2013/e0707r.pdf, 8.

HLF trial, FBI Special Agent Lara Burns labeled CAIR "a front group for Hamas," a serious accusation against the credibility of the organization.[19] Despite this, CAIR presents itself as a leading civil rights organization and denies any ties to the Muslim Brotherhood, a stark contrast to its designation as a terrorist organization by Saudi Arabia, Egypt, and the U.A.E. France's lower chamber of parliament, in a positive development, passed a resolution[20] in January 2026 categorizing the Muslim Brotherhood in the same manner—a terrorist organization—citing its "subversive ideology, its backing of terrorist entities like Hamas, its calls for hatred, and its covert action against democratic institutions."[21]

The ambiguity in CAIR's strategy, which reflects Sun Tzu's use of deception, allows its leaders to traffic in un-American and antisemitic rhetoric. Nihad Awad, CAIR's executive director and a former figure in the Holy Land Foundation, notably stated in 2014 that "Israel is the greatest threat to world peace and security."[22] Following the events of October 7, Awad claimed that Israel did not possess the right to defend itself after the attack, expressing his "happiness" to see "people breaking

19. U.S. Government Publishing Office, "Identifying the Enemy—Radical Islamist Terror," House of Representatives Hearing, 114 Congress, September 22, 2016, www.govinfo.gov/content/pkg/CHRG-114hhrg25270/html/CHRG-114hhrg25270.htm.

20. Assemblée Nationale, "Résolution visant à inscrire la mouvance des Frères musulmans sur la liste européenne des organisations terroristes le 22 janvier 2026, T.A. n° 215," 17e législature, January 22, 2026, www.assemblee-nationale.fr/dyn/17/textes/l17t0215_texte-adopte-seance.

21. Jules Gomes, "France's National Assembly Votes to Designate Muslim Brotherhood as Terrorist Organization," *Middle East Forum* (Focus on Western Islamism), January 26, 2026, www.meforum.org/fwi/fwi-news/frances-national-assembly-votes-to-designate-muslim-brotherhood-a-terrorist-organization.

22. The Investigative Project on Terrorism, "CAIR Chief—Never Mind ISIS, "Israel Is The Biggest Threat To World Peace,'" *Breitbart*, August 22, 2014, www.breitbart.com/national-security/2014/08/22/cair-chief-israel-greatest-threat/.

the siege."[23] Other CAIR leaders, such as Zahra Billoo, executive director of CAIR–San Francisco Bay Area, further escalated this rhetoric by declaring "Zionists" as "your enemies," further warning followers to "pay attention" to "Zionist synagogues" and other notable Jewish American organizations.[24] Awad and Billoo are among many CAIR officials frequently accused of spreading antisemitism and inciting hatred and violence in American society.

With an annual budget exceeding $2 million, offices established in some 20 states, a network of over 60 chapters, and more than 300 active volunteer board or executive committee members, CAIR possesses a formidable arsenal regarding its own infrastructure.[25] On the academic front, CAIR has a history of defending hostile anti-Israel encampments at U.S. universities, including designating institutions like George Washington University as a "hostile campus" for their attempts to restrict pro-Hamas activism led by SJP.[26] Furthermore, the group uses its legal resources to support SJP chapters and individual activists facing disciplinary action

---

23. Anti-Defamation League, "The Council on American Islamic Relations (CAIR)," Anti-Defamation League, n.d., www.adl.org/resources/backgrounder/council-american-islamic-relations-cair?gad_source=1&gad_campaignid=10844164222&gbraid=0AAAAADtja52lGok3qfZ_agc4Dw-fMqDLrU&gclid=Cj0KCQjw-ZHEBhCxARIsAGGN96ICQMh2A1h-23K0yHJ5Kr-7O1D5TJ6tvCq4ta4Meok-RKLAfsjY1KdUaAphqEALw_wc-B&gclsrc=aw.ds.

24. Combat Antisemitism Movement, "Zahra Billoo's Hateful Speech Reinforces CAIR's Antisemitism Problem," Combat Antisemitism Movement, December 16, 2021, combatantisemitism.org/cam-news/zahra-billoos-hateful-speech-reinforces-cairs-antisemitism-problem/.

25. Canary Mission, "Council on American Islamic Relations," *Canary Mission*, n.d., canarymission.org/organization/Council_On_American_Islamic_Relations

26. Council on American-Islamic Relations (CAIR), "Hostile Campuses: George Washington University," Islamophobia.org, islamophobia.org/hostile-campuses/hostile-campuses-george-washington-university/.

or arrest, framing university efforts as suppressing free speech and enforcing anti-Muslim discrimination.[27] Here, CAIR flips reality in classic Orwellian fashion. Universities trying to maintain order and stability, protect Jewish students from harassment, and enforce neutral conduct rules are branded "Islamophobic." While CAIR treats dissent from SJP's preferred narrative as a thoughtcrime, it fails to recognize that equating the enforcement of university rules with "suppression of free speech" is a form of doublethink. Indeed, while CAIR often defends Muslims from civil rights violations and champions the rights of Muslims to express their beliefs in the civil sphere, it is selective in its application of free speech principles when it comes to criticism of Hamas. In October 2024, CAIR successfully sued the University of Maryland for denying SJP a permit for a pro-Hamas vigil on October 7.[28]

Behind its public façade, the organization includes a strong lobbying strategy designed to influence local, state, and national leaders working to topple the U.S.-Israel alliance. The group regularly issues "action alerts," encouraging readers to send prepared letters to members of Congress to either approve or oppose specific pro-Israel legislation, and publishes press releases and op-eds to ensure its leaders can shape public discourse on current affairs. CAIR's operations in other realms of the civil sphere follow a typical Islamist pattern, which aims to prevent the U.S. government from cracking down on Muslim Brotherhood–related

27. Council on American-Islamic Relations, "CAIR and CAIR–Chicago Designate University of Illinois Urbana—Champaign (UIUC) as 'Hostile Campus' for Targeting Anti-Genocide Voices," Council on American-Islamic Relations–Chicago, n.d., www.cairchicago.org/blog/cair-and-cair-chicago-designate-university-of-illinois-urbana-champaign-uiuc-ashostile-campusfor-targeting-anti-genocide-voices.

28. Larry Estavan, "CAIR Wins Legal Battle for SJP Leftists," *Middle East Forum*, October 7, 2024, www.meforum.org/fwi/fwi-news/cair-to-comment/cair-wins-legal-battle-for-sjp-leftists#.

radicalization.[29] This extensive network of chapters and leaders, functioning as a network of "knights," is able to control the public discourse and protect CAIR's ideological realm from opposing narratives presented by the U.S.-Israel alliance.

More troubling is that CAIR has received federal funding from entities like the Department of Homeland Security (DHS). A 2025 report from the Middle East Forum (MEF) revealed that CAIR received nearly $250,000 in DHS security grants for its national office and its chapters in Los Angeles and Miami.[30] The MEF report raises serious questions about how Islamist groups such as CAIR have successfully manipulated the government to receive federal funding, which the report claims is a tactic often used by these groups to recruit and radicalize new followers. Organizations like the MEF are crucial in exposing government abuse, fraud, and waste. Its work ensures that taxpayer dollars intended for safety are not used to fund intolerance or something worse, like terrorism.

My own relationship with CAIR has changed significantly over the years, transforming from initial positive engagement to a stark realization of its role within the Leftist-Islamist alliance. In my early years as a lecturer at Rice, my relationship with CAIR was amicable. I invited CAIR leaders to speak in my classes and openly defended the organization in my books, rejecting claims that it was a terrorist organization. I viewed such claims as nothing more than smears from the "Islamophobia industry."[31] My engagement with the organization even intersected

---

29. Jerusalem Center for Security and Foreign Affairs, "Islamist Organizations," n.d., jcpa.org/the-spiders-web/chapter-iv-delegitimization-in-the-united-states/islamist-organizations/.

30. Middle East Forum, "MEF Report Reveals DHS Hands Millions to Terrorist-Linked Groups," *Middle East Forum*, July 21, 2025, www.meforum.org/press-releases/mef-report-reveals-dhs-hands-millions-to-terrorist-linked-groups.

31. Craig Considine. *Islam in America—Exploring the Issues* (New York: Bloomsbury, 2019).

with CAIR's broader public platform, with CAIR publishing my article, "What Studying Muhammad Taught Me About Islam," on its website, where it remains as of this writing.

My second-to-last direct encounter with CAIR occurred in 2022, when one of my then-friends, an Egyptian American local leader at the Multicultural Center (MCC) in Houston, invited me to a "civic event" at the center. Prior to my speech, the MCC honored me with its annual Community Bridge Builder Award. During the event, I noticed Nihad Awad, CAIR's founder, in attendance, having encountered him a few times over the years. Even though, at the time, I believed that claims linking CAIR to the Muslim Brotherhood were smear tactics, I still wanted to be careful with my words, and I publicly acknowledged that CAIR did important work in addressing legitimate civil rights claims and protecting the rights of Muslim Americans. My stance has always been one that promotes religious freedom, so long as that freedom does not impinge on the freedoms of others, and I am against any kind of religious supremacy, whether Christian or Islamic, that infringes on the rights of others. Like many outside of CAIR's inside circle who follow such a guiding principle, I was blinded to the true nature of CAIR's work and the intricate web of affiliations within the Leftist-Islamist alliance.

The last direct encounter I had with CAIR followed my subsequent vocal condemnations of the pro-Hamas protests and my growing awareness of my own blindness toward the ideological alignment between various Leftist and Islamist groups. The CAIR–Houston chapter leader publicly blasted me on X for being a "traitor" and essentially a "snake," echoing the same claim made by Nathan Lean, as noted in the previous chapter. They, like many others in the Leftist-Islamist alliance, suggested that I had been "bought by 'Zionists'" and that I had "deceived everyone over the years." This aggressive response from a key CAIR figure shows the clear ideological line in the sand: you are "approved" if you praise Islam and Islamist organizations, as I had done in previous years, but you are "condemned" the minute you extend even the modest support for Israel over the Palestinian cause. By publicly discrediting voices that advocate for Israel or even simply challenge the "Free Palestine" movement's methods, CAIR effectively creates an environment where SJP and similar organizations can operate with some level of impunity, because their words and actions are framed as legitimate civil rights advocacy, even when they veer into blatant antisemitism if not overt support of terrorist organizations.

Over time, it became clear that if anyone was deceived regarding CAIR, it was me— deceived by what I now understand to be the group's direct role within the Leftist-Islamist alliance. This experience demonstrates how CAIR, through its leadership, actively supports Hamas's agenda, aligning itself with the broader Leftist-Islamist alliance and its opposition to Israel and its allies. The group's rhetorical attacks on me and other individuals who challenge antisemitism serve to reinforce and empower student activist groups, providing them with the necessary resources and moral support to realize their radical agenda.

JEWISH VOICE FOR PEACE AND THE BETRAYAL OF JEWISH VALUES: UNPACKING THE "JEWISH" FACE OF ANTI-ZIONISM

The Trojan Horse, as we have seen, is a favored tactic of the Leftist-Islamist alliance in its "soft war" against the West in general and the U.S.-Israel alliance in particular. The first chapter, for example, showed that "neutral" and open environments such as academic campuses, where free inquiry is supposed to reign, are susceptible to internal subversion. Matters are compounded further when that hypothetical horse is wheeled into the very sanctuary it seeks to undermine, disguised not merely as a gift, like in the case of Troy, but as a symbol of faith.

If SJP represents the mobilized student arm of a broader radical, pro-Hamas ideology, then Jewish Voice for Peace (JVP), a prominent anti-Zionist organization, serves as its ideological shield by cloaking Marxist ideology in Jewish identity. The group blames Israel for both Jewish and Palestinian suffering, claims that Zionism is "racist" and a product of "white supremacy," and believes that a "utopian future" will come with the destruction of the Jewish state.[32] With these tactics, JVP repurposes Jewishness not as a source of solidarity, but as a political tool, one that reinforces ideologies rooted in hostility to Enlightenment principles, American values, and Israel itself. It also provides a veneer of legitimacy to radical Islamist groups and shields them from accusations of antisemitism.

JVP's response to October 7 was to blame Israel, not Hamas, for the attack, claiming that Israel is "the source of all this violence" and that "Israeli apartheid and occupation," along with "[American] complicity in that oppression," were the true source of the conflict.[33] Critics see this response as an act of antisemitic inversion and historical revisionism. In blaming Israel, JVP abandoned the principles of moral clarity and reasoned debate, which are paramount not only to Jewish identity but also to building a healthy democratic society, as a civic culture requires a respect for facts and a willingness to condemn terrorism. There is also something akin to Holocaust denial in JVP's October 7 response, as it hinges upon the belief that Jews exaggerate, manufacture, and misrepresent Jewish suffering for their own individual and collective gains.

The situation in the British context is similar. Jewish Voice for Liberation (JVL), formerly Jewish Voice for Labor, and Jewish Network for Palestine (JNP) are Leftist British organizations positioning themselves as Jewish-led groups supporting anti-Zionism, viewing it as a form of

32. Jewish Voice for Peace, "Our Approach to Zionism," n.d., www.jewishvoiceforpeace.org/resource/zionism/.

33. Jewish Voice for Peace, "The Root of Violence Is Oppression," n.d., www.jewishvoiceforpeace.org/2023/10/07/statement23-10-07/

"settler-colonialism" and an "apartheid state" guilty of "genocide" in Gaza and the West Bank. While many British Jews regard JVL as a fringe group within the national Jewish community, its activism still provides a shield for radical Islamist groups who overtly promote antisemitism. On the German front, Jüdische Stimme für gerechten Frieden in Nahost (Jewish Voice for a Just Peace in the Middle East) is another anti-Zionist Jewish organization that fits the pattern of groups like JVP, JVL, and JNP. Unsurprisingly, Jüdische Stimme für gerechten Frieden works to "decolonize" the Middle East from Israeli control, end the "apartheid" system in Israel, and put an immediate end to "ethnic cleansing" in Palestine. All these organizations capture the absurdity, perverse inversion, and betrayal of a critical part of the Leftist-Islamist alliance, with Jewish individuals actively shielding and legitimizing groups whose foundational charters and actions are explicitly antisemitic.

JVP's chapters around the country are active on college campuses and on U.S. streets. In February 2024, the JVP chapter at Hunter College co-sponsored a protest in which protesters were heard chanting, "We say no to genocide, Jews on campus pick a side."[34] These chants not only echoed age-old antisemitic tropes accusing Jews of disloyalty, but also played into the Manichaean binary and Marxist framework of there being only two sides. At a similar May 2021 rally in New York City organized by JVP and AMP, among other Leftist and Islamist organizations, a protester held a sign reading, "The Nazis are still around, they just call themselves Zionists now."[35] This comparison of equating Zionists and Jews who support Israel with Nazis is an act of antisemitic

---

34. Luke Tress, "NY's Hunter College investigates after protesters demand Jews on campus 'pick a side,'" *Times of Israel*, March 2, 2024, www.timesofisrael.com/nys-hunter-college-investigates-after-protesters-demand-jews-on-campus-pick-a-side/.

35. Anti-Defamation League, "Jewish Voice for Peace," updated March 23, 2026, www.adl.org/resources/backgrounder/jewish-voice-peace-jvp.

inversion and historical revisionism, all too powerful themes arising out of Orwell's *Animal Farm* and *Nineteen Eighty-Four*. These Marxist and Orwellian tactics allow "civil society" groups like JVP to use their Jewish identity to shield groups like SJP and others in the anti-American and anti-Israel movement from allegations of antisemitism.[36] With thousands of member-volunteers, these "knights" on the chessboard protect the "pawns" and "bishops" from attacks on the ideological battlefield.

The financial backbone of JVP anchors its role as a key player in the Leftist-Islamist alliance. According to publicly available tax filings, JVP's 501(c)(3) arm reported a massive increase in revenue from 2023 to 2024, growing from $3,322,296 to $11,003,649.[37] In January 2025, the Attorney's Office in Washington, D.C., announced that JVP would be obligated to pay $677,634 to settle allegations that the organization violated the False Claims Act, a U.S. federal law imposing liability on individuals or companies who defraud governmental programs.[38] This settlement highlights the gravity of concerns surrounding JVP's finances and even its operational integrity. In addition, AMP, the patron of SJP, has admitted to providing some funding to JVP.[39] Critically important going forward, JVP members voted in 2025 to restructure the organization as a 501(c)(4). Although JVP will continue to have a 501(c)(3)

36. Ibid.

37. "Jewish Voice for Peace Leadership and Culture Lab," ProPublica, projects.propublica.org/nonprofits/organizations/900018359.

38. U.S. Attorney's Office–District of Columbia, "Non-Profit A Jewish Voice for Peace, Inc. to Pay $677,634 to Resolve PPP Fraud Allegations," U.S. Attorney's Office—District of Columbia, January 14, 2025, www.justice.gov/usao-dc/pr/non-profit-jewish-voice-peace-inc-pay-677634-resolve-ppp-fraud-allegations

39. Charles Asher Small, "Fueling Chaos—Tracing the Flow of Tax-Exempt Dollars to Antisemitism," United States House Committee on Ways and Means, July 23, 2024, waysandmeans.house.gov/wp-content/uploads/2024/07/Small-Testimony.pdf.

arm, this move will allow it to focus even more on political organizing, to have even greater involvement in elections and legislation, and to lend increased support to candidates aligned with anti-Israel stances.[40] In the lead-up to Zohran Mamdani's mayoral victory, for example, JVP Action, JVP's then 501(c)(4) arm, claims to have organized, trained, and sent more than 5,000 volunteers to knock on 200,000 doors in New York City.[41]

While JVP brands itself as an advocate of Jewish values, human rights, and peace, its activities and alliances have raised concern among the majority of Jewish Americans. According to the Anti-Defamation League, JVP does not represent the mainstream Jewish community, which views it as misguided, if not bigoted.[42] While I have had no direct contact or confrontation with the organization, my experiences growing up in Needham, Massachusetts, a town with a substantial and engaged Jewish community, accustomed me to aspects of liberal Jewish thought—one committed to "social justice," but unequivocally supportive of Israel's right to exist as a Jewish state, even while criticizing the policies of the Israeli government. It is with a significant dose of wisdom gained from my previous experiences that I now observe how groups like JVP have strayed from those principles.

As we move beyond this organization into the "knights" of the wider activist Left, we find similarly aligned groups like Black Lives Matter, the People's Forum, and Code Pink—entities that not only share SJP and JVP's worldview, but also have troubling ties to authoritarian international actors.

40. Anti-Defamation League, "Jewish Voice for Peace (JVP)," Anti-Defamation League, n.d., www.adl.org/resources/backgrounder/jewish-voice-peace-jvp.

41. "JVP Action and the Road to Zohran Mamdani's Historic Victory," n.d., www.jvpaction.org/roadtozohran/.

42. Anti-Defamation League, "Jewish Voice for Peace (JVP)."

THE BLACK LIVES MATTER NEXUS: SHARED IDEOLOGY, SHARED REVOLUTION

One of the most puzzling assertions of the Leftist-Islamist alliance, yet a cornerstone of its ambitions, is the claim that all perceived injustices across the world are but threads woven into a single tapestry of "oppression" orchestrated by "Western capitalism" (i.e., the U.S. and Israel). While the impacts of globalization—from financial markets to oil prices to international wars—demonstrate a clear interconnectedness of the world, it is an intellectually specious leap to claim that the plight of Palestinians in Gaza is inherently linked to the struggles faced by African Americans. This insistence on a singular, universal, and interconnected struggle, despite the unique historical episodes and societal contexts, demands, according to the Leftist-Islamist alliance, a "global revolution" across the West and throughout the Middle East.

The alliance between Black Lives Matter (BLM), the focus of this section, and Islamist factions becomes obvious in considering their shared ideology and enemies. The co-founder of BLM, Alicia Garza, made her Marxist views clear when she stated that BLM seeks to "chang[e] how we've organized [American society]," stressing that Americans need to dismantle their institutions and radically transform civil society.[43] In 2015, she defended Marxism and communism, telling *San Francisco Weekly* that "social movements all over the world have used Marx and Lenin as a foundation to interrupt these systems that are really negatively impacting the majority of the people."[44] In 2019, she reiterated her

43. Dan Neumann, "Black Lives Matter Co-Founder Can Be a Leader in Dismantling White Nationalism," *Maine Beacon*, June 28, 2019, mainebeacon.com/black-lives-matter-co-founder-maine-can-be-a-leader-in-dismantling-white-nationalism/.

44. San Francisco Weekly, "The Bay Area Roots of Black Lives Matter," *San Francisco Weekly*, November 11, 2015, www.sfweekly.com/archives/the-bay-area-roots-of-black-lives-matter/article_59c2bc82-80c4-5b2b-9600-28c62c8b-

Marxist agenda when she told an audience in Maine, "We are talking about changing how we have organized this country, so that we actually can achieve the justice that we are fighting for," adding, "I believe we all have work to do to keep dismantling the organizing principle of this society, which creates inequities for everyone, even white people."[45] Calling for systemic dismantling of "systems," a stance rooted in Marxist thought, is the revolutionary imperative of BLM and its allies within the Leftist-Islamist alliance.

The deaths of African Americans at the hands of police officers have become catalysts that reveal deeper connections between Marxist-inspired movements like Black Lives Matter and pro-Palestinian groups. Michael Brown's death in Ferguson, Missouri, in 2014 transformed the city into a temporary epicenter of global Marxism, becoming a battleground in the "soft war."[46] After the death of George Floyd in 2020, the BLM-Islamist coalition reached a pinnacle during the "George Floyd riots," during which at least 25 Americans were killed and rioters caused an estimated $2 billion worth of property damage.[47] According to the Property Claim Services, those riots were "the costliest civil disorder in [American] history."[48] BLM activists participated in 95 percent of the

---

29fb.html.

45. Neumann, "Black Lives Matter Co-Founder Can Be a Leader in Dismantling White Nationalism."

46. Mike Gonzalez, "BLM and Palestinian Groups Are Cut From the Same Radical Cloth," *The Heritage Foundation*, October 30, 2023, www.heritage.org/progressivism/commentary/blm-and-palestinian-groups-are-cut-the-same-radical-cloth.

47. Lois Beckett, "At Least 25 Americans Were Killed During Protests and Political Unrest in 2020," *The Guardian*, October 31, 2020, www.theguardian.com/world/2020/oct/31/americans-killed-protests-political-unrest-acled

48. Jennifer A. Kingson, "Exclusive - $1 billion-plus riot damage is most expensive in insurance history," *Axios*, September 16, 2020, www.axios.com/2020/09/16/riots-cost-property-damage.

633 incidents that the Armed Conflict Location and Event Data Project identified as riots in which the identity of participants was known.[49] The riots embodied the triumph of Marxism over Enlightenment values. Isolated tragedies were turned into pretexts for widespread violence in which "mob justice" and "by any means necessary" appeared to supersede the "rule of law" and "peaceful reform."

Following Brown's death in Ferguson, another convergence occurred when a prominent group of African American activists, artists, musicians, and journalists ventured to the Palestinian territories and Israel in January 2015. These Ferguson "foot soldiers" and members of the burgeoning BLM movement embarked on a ten-day trip, joining forces with "Dream Defenders," a nonprofit organization and the primary organizer of the venture. The Dream Defenders co-founder, Ahmad Abuznai, a Palestinian American lawyer, linked the group's aims to the spirit of prominent African American leaders, emphasizing the need to "reestablish and fortify" connections between African American leaders and Palestinians, framing their shared cause in military terms.[50] Abuznai referred specifically to Malcolm X and Angela Davis, a leading member of the Communist Party USA in the late 1960s and early 1970s, as two exemplars for the Leftist-Islamist alliance in this particular "battle," showing how Islamist organizations co-opt the "heroes" of Leftist movements for their own agenda.

A co-founder of BLM—Patrisse Cullors—returned from the trip

---

49. Joy Pullmann, "Study—Up to 95 Percent Of 2020 U.S. Riots Are Linked to Black Lives Matter," *The Federalist*, September 16, 2020, thefederalist.com/2020/09/16/study-up-to-95-percent-of-2020-u-s-riots-are-linked-to-black-lives-matter/.

50. #Teambony, "Dream Defenders, Black Lives Matter And Ferguson Reps Take Historic Trip To Palestine," *Ebony*, January 9, 2015, www.ebony.com/dream-defenders-black-lives-matter-ferguson-reps-take-historic-trip-to-palestine/#axzz3OrNLQBby.

and claimed that "[Israel] is an apartheid state. We cannot deny that, and if we do deny it, we are part of the Zionist violence."[51] This quote captures several sociological concepts described in the previous chapters. We see Orwellianism in the call for "ideological conformity," Marxism in the perceived "oppressive system," and Fanonism in the call for "liberation." We also see elements of critical race theory (CRT), whereby Cullors suggested that any individual who fails to side with the Palestinians automatically makes one complicit in the alleged violence, which amounts to "collective guilt," or in this specific case, "white guilt." She is also on record stating that American society requires a "complete transformation [across] all branches of government" to alter the fate of the country.[52]

Cherrell Brown, a "community organizer" who also participated in the Dream Defenders mission, provided her perspective of the trip, claiming that the "oppressors" of African Americans and Palestinians are "literally collaborating together . . . and as oppressed people we have to do the same."[53] Upon her return to the United States, she hoped to "reimagine what society could and will look like when we have dismantled this white-supremacist patriarchal and capitalist society."[54] As with Cullors's statements, Brown's aims and worldview are intertwined with elements of Marxism, Orwellianism, and CRT, aligning seamlessly with the objectives of certain Islamist movements. Her Marxist vision calls for "revolution," the dismantlement of existing systems, and the reali-

---

51. Ibid.

52. Patrisse Cullors and Darnell I. Moore, "Ferguson Protest to #FergusonNext. 5 Paths to Progress After Non-Indictment," *The Guardian*, November 24, 2014, www.theguardian.com/commentisfree/2014/nov/24/ferguson-protests-progress-non-indictment-grand-jury

53. #Teambony, "Dream Defenders, Black Lives Matter And Ferguson Reps Take Historic Trip To Palestine."

54. Ibid.

zation of a utopian future. An Orwellian perspective is seen in Brown's framing, compelling Americans to accept a prescribed reality or face condemnation and public shaming. CRT's influence is evident in her identification of "white supremacy" as a primary target, her description of racism as "pervasive," her redefining of racism as a "system," and her overall activist language. These Manichaean frameworks, dividing the world into "black" and "white," leave scant room for gradual change. Instead, they cultivate a culture in which dissenting views are treated as "thoughtcrime" rather than as opportunities for dialogue. Predictably, Islamists readily embrace these positions, as their identified "oppressors"—capitalism, colonization, secularization, and "white supremacy"—align with those on the Left.

The convergence of BLM with Palestinian solidarity efforts is also evident on campuses across the United States. In May 2021, the Massachusetts Institute of Technology Arab Alumni Association hosted an online seminar featuring activists Marc Lamont Hill, who participated in the Dream Defenders trip, and Mohammed El-Kurd, a Palestinian writer from East Jerusalem and the West Bank.[55] This webinar centered on "fighting oppression," asserting that there are numerous parallels between the struggle of Palestinians and African Americans against "state violence, institutionalized racism, and settler colonialism in the U.S. and Occupied Palestine, where decades of anti-Palestinian and anti-Black violence are at the core of both countries' foundations."[56] The "state violence, institutionalized racism, and settler colonialism" outlined in the webinar's description aligns with the perspectives of Marx and Fanon, who posited that the material conditions of dispossession, poverty, and

55. Massachusetts Institute of Technology—Black History, "From Ferguson to Sheikh Jarrah—The Black and Palestinian Struggle for Justice (2021)," Massachusetts Institute of Technology, n.d., www.blackhistory.mit.edu/archive/ferguson-sheikh-jarrah-black-and-palestinian-struggle-justice-2021.

56. Ibid.

limited opportunities for marginalized groups reinforced their subordinate positions within the capitalist system. Furthermore, Gramsci's concept of hegemony and Said's critique of hegemonic narratives are central to the event's description, noting that a society's primary systems perpetuate a "dominant ideology" that imposes and justifies "systematic oppression." The session further explored "alternative viewpoints on the historical context of systematic racism inherent in the Israeli occupation in Palestine and anti-Blackness" in America, emphasizing that "joint solidarity across struggles is key for liberation." This part of the description reflects Orwellian themes, especially concerning the control of historical narratives and the suppression of truth as tools for maintaining power.

The "solidarity" between Palestinians and African Americans also plays out in reverse. In November 2014, a group of ten Palestinian student activists from Birzeit University, located in the West Bank, participated in the "Right to Education Campaign."[57] The group visited Ferguson, met with local leaders, and "organized" in the streets. A month later, upon their return, these student activists hosted a series of events at their university in the West Bank to raise awareness of the African American struggle and to "stand in solidarity"[58] with African Americans. The ongoing collaboration between BLM and Palestinian groups that advance Leftist-Islamist narratives further underscores their shared ideological foundations and strategic alignment.

European countries have also grappled with the rise of BLM and its collaboration with Palestinian advocacy groups. This paired activism—framing both causes through lenses of settler colonialism, systemic

---

57. Rania Khalek, "Watch—Ferguson activists bring message of 'love and struggle' to Palestine," *Electronic Intifada*, January 16, 2015, electronicintifada.net/blogs/rania-khalek/watch-ferguson-activists-bring-message-love-and-struggle-palestine.

58. #Teambony, "Dream Defenders, Black Lives Matter And Ferguson Reps Take Historic Trip To Palestine."

oppression, and state violence—has imported American-style identity politics into European contexts, often linking Leftist "antiracism" campaigns with pro-Palestinian solidarity. In France, this approach clashes with the core republican motto of liberté, égalité, fraternité. The French republican tradition of color-blind universalism frames all citizens as equal individuals without regard to ethnicity, group identity, or race, making it fundamentally opposed to BLM ideology, which emphasizes race-based or structural racism rather than individual prejudice. As a result, BLM-Palestine advocacy groups frequently express disdain for France's motto, viewing its refusal to acknowledge "systemic" racism as a form of denial that protects the status quo. French authorities and many public intellectuals, in turn, sometimes portray BLM tactics and the broader "decolonization" framework as "un-French" and an unnecessary American import that threatens national unity by promoting Leftist ideology over universal republican values.

I experienced the reality of BLM's ideological underpinnings firsthand during an interaction in my more left-leaning days, when I reached out to the BLM–Houston chapter to invite a representative to speak to my students at Rice about the burgeoning BLM movement. The local activist that I connected with was pleasant in our initial communication on Twitter (now X). He expressed a willingness to speak but stipulated a small stipend. While an honorarium is a common request for speakers, his response carried a discernible edge of anger. He stated that the days of African Americans doing "unpaid labor" were "long gone." I was admittedly taken aback by this comment, as it suggested that I, a white man, was attempting to exploit him, a black man. This was certainly not my intention, yet his immediate framing of the interaction through the lens of "racialized labor" and "historical exploitation" is a classic application of Marxism and CRT, where racial power dynamics are presumed to be at play in every interaction. Despite my surprise, I provided him with $100 for two talks that day.

During his appearance in my class, the topic of reparations arose. At that time, I supported the idea of reparations for descendants of African Americans and Native Americans. However, my view was that it needed to be a systematic approach, far more than a "handout," ensuring these groups could sustain long-term capital gain. My perspective on reparations began to shift with my growing critique of the anti-colonial movement, a subject I found problematic and biased for focusing solely on "Western colonization." While there is no question that African Americans and Native Americans endured uniquely inhumane treatment in American history, the CRT framework focused solely on the white and non-white binary, which prompts important questions: What about other marginalized groups who suffered religious and racial discrimination, such as the Irish, Italian, and Jewish people in the nineteenth century? Are these groups neglected in the discussion on reparations simply because, according to CRT orthodoxy, they "became white"? This selective focus on certain historical grievances, while overlooking others, highlights the limitations and potential for clear double standards within the Leftist-Islamist alliance.

BLM, with its Marxist worldview and selective application of historical grievances, provides strategic support and offers cover for an agenda aimed at weakening the West in general and the U.S.-Israel alliance in particular. However, it is certainly not the only U.S.-based Marxist organization operating in the West.

THE PEOPLE'S FORUM AND CODE PINK: FOREIGN AGENDAS AND CONGRESSIONAL SCRUTINY

These domestic networks are further amplified by organizations with clear ties to foreign powers. The People's Forum (TPF) stands out as another key organization in the "soft war," a "knight" that embodies the convergence of Marxist ideologies and the Islamist agenda. TPF bills itself, according to its website, as a "movement incubator for working class and marginalized communities" that "nurtures the next generation of visionaries and organizers who believe that through collective action a new world is possible." While it presents itself as a hub for the "working class" (i.e., the proletariat, in Marxist terms) by organizing protests and cultural events, the group advocates for radical social change within the larger "anti-imperialist" movement in the West. A clear illustration is that one day after October 7, 2023, TPF shared a post on X that encouraged the mobilization of its "troops" in New York to go "all out for Palestine," urging supporters to "resist apartheid, occupation, and oppression."[59]

TPF's executive director, Manolo De Los Santos, has forged a career out of inciting protests across New York City while openly advancing Hamas's interests on American soil. Particularly active at Columbia University,[60] De Los Santos stood alongside Palestinian activist and Columbia student Mahmoud Khalil in June 2025, shortly after Khalil's release from ICE detention. In his speech, Khalil accused U.S. Secretary of State Marco Rubio of regularly meeting with "new Nazis," a clear reference to pro-Israel Jews and their supporters.[61] Earlier, in January 2024,

59. Eric Revell, "American multimillionaire couple funds Marxist group coordinating anti-Israel protests," *Fox News Business*, November 15, 2023, www.foxbusiness.com/politics/american-multimillionaire-couple-fund-marxist-group-coordinating-anti-israel-protests.

60. Jack Morphet and Chris Nesi, "Who Is Manolo De Los Santos? Leader of Hamas-Cheering Radical NYC Group Has Ties to Cuba," *New York Post*, May 6, 2024, nypost.com/2024/05/06/us-news/who-is-manolo-de-los-santos-leader-of-hamas-cheering-radical-nyc-group-has-ties-to-cuba/.

61. Middle East Media Research Institute, "Columbia University Pro-Palestinian Activist Mahmoud Khalil in Rally to Celebrate His Release from ICE Detention—They Claim My Words Undermine U.S. Policy to Combat Antisemitism, but Israel Is the Top Threat to U.S. Foreign Policy; U.S. Government Is a Killing Machine; Crowd Chants—'There Is Only One Solution—Intifada,

De Los Santos was among ten protest leaders detained during a "day of anarchy" in which anti-Israel demonstrations partially blocked the Brooklyn Bridge and attempted to shut down traffic at John F. Kennedy Airport.

To emphasize an important point, De Los Santos's radicalism extends beyond mere protest. Notably, he traveled to Cuba, a communist country, in 2006 and again as recently as March 2024 to denounce "American hegemony" and demand an end to the U.S. blockade on Cuba that has been in place since 1962.[62] His leadership at TPF embodies the strategic convergence of radical Marxist ideologies and Islamist agendas. He utilizes anti-capitalist, anti-imperialist, and anti-Zionist narratives to fuel disruptive activism.

De Los Santos's extremist views surfaced at the height of the 2023–24 pro-Palestinian protests in the United States when he was recorded stating, "When we finally deal that final blow to destroy Israel, when the state of Israel is finally destroyed and erased from history, that will be the single most important blow we can give to destroying capitalism and imperialism in our lifetime."[63] These remarks draw a parallel to Nazi rhetoric about a "final solution," a kind of genocidal ideology that the TPF has been caught promoting as the "final blow." When confronted by the *New York Post* about his organization's role in protests, De Los Santos offered a deflective statement, rejecting characterizations of violence and instead blaming the police as the true "source of the violence."[64] His response is Orwellian, manipulating truth by shifting blame and denying documented realities, a common tactic used to discredit opposition and

---

Revolution!" *Middle East Media Research Institute*, June 22, 2025, www.memri.org/tv/mahmoud-khalil-rally-us-killing-machine-israel-threat.

62. Ibid.

63. The People's Forum New York City, Instagram, post dated December 6, 2023, www.instagram.com/p/C0hWpCJAFTK/.

64. Morphet and Nesi, "Who Is Manolo De Los Santos?"

control narratives.

Beyond the rhetoric and its on-the-ground disruptions, TPF reportedly has significant financial backing from Roy Neville Singham, a wealthy businessperson whose extensive network actively pushes a radical agenda that aligns with Islamist groups like Hamas. Singham is noted[65] for funding the Progress Unity Fund, which in turn sponsors both TPF and the broader "Shut It Down for Palestine" (SID4P) movement, an activist coalition focused on disrupting or halting the activities of political offices, businesses, and workplaces with ties to Israel.[66] Singham's extensive network includes various nonprofits, fiscal sponsors, and news sources, notably the Chinese Communist Party (CCP)–connected BreakThrough News, which has been the subject of numerous investigations linked to foreign agencies. According to a report from the Network Contagion Research Institute (NCRI), Singham's network acts as "the conduit through which CCP-affiliated entities have effectively co-opted pro-Palestinian activism ... advancing a broader anti-American, anti-democratic, and anti-capitalist agenda."[67] This connection extends to the highest levels of foreign influence. As a *New York Times* report revealed, Singham "works closely with the Chinese government media

---

65. U.S. House of Representatives Committee on Natural Resources, "Desecrating Old Glory—Investigating How the Pro-Hamas Protests Turned National Park Service Land into a Violent Disgrace," U.S. House of Representatives Committee on Natural Resources, December 10, 2024, www.congress.gov/118/chrg/CHRG-118hhrg57751/CHRG-118hhrg57751.pdf, x.

66. Influence Watch, "Shut It Down for Palestine (SID4P)," *Influence Watch*, n.d., www.influencewatch.org/organization/shut-it-down-for-palestine-sid4p/.

67. Network Contagion Research Institute, "Contagious Disruption—How CCP Influence and Radical Ideologies Threaten Critical Infrastructure and Campuses Across the United States," *Network Contagion Research Institute*, May 2024, networkcontagion.us/wp-content/uploads/SID4P-Report_May-2024.pdf.

machine and is financing its propaganda worldwide."[68]

A prime example of Singham's orchestrated effort is *The Encampments*, a documentary produced in 2025.[69] The film, backed by BreakThrough News, portrays the campus protests in a positive light, conveniently glossing over the students' support for Hamas. Instead, it glorifies them as heroic "resisters," omitting the well-documented antisemitic incidents and open endorsements for terrorism during the protests. BreakThrough News's popular YouTube channel features interviews with members of the Popular Front for the Liberation of Palestine (PFLP), a designated Palestinian communist terrorist group, and episodes with inflammatory titles such as "How the Pro-Israel Lobby Hijacked Judaism."[70] Key figures behind *The Encampments* further solidify the radical alignment between Leftists and Islamists. Ben Becker, the editor-in-chief of BreakThrough News, is the executive producer, with acknowledged contributions from BreakThrough News host Eugene Puryear. Both Becker and Puryear are co-founders of the Party for Socialism and Liberation, a far-left "progressive" organization whose past affiliates included Elias Rodriguez, the Marxist who killed Yaron Lischinsky and Sarah Milgrim. The former publicly defended Hamas's actions on October 7 as an act of "national liberation against colonial-

---

68. Mara Hvistendahl, David A. Fahrenthold, Lynsey Chutel, and Ishaan Jhaveri, "A Global Web of Chinese Propaganda Leads to a U.S. Tech Mogul," *New York Times*, August 10, 2023, www.nytimes.com/2023/08/05/world/europe/neville-roy-singham-china-propaganda.html.

69. Chuck Ross, "An Anti-American Propaganda Network Encouraged Violent Protests at Columbia—Then Produced a Documentary Lauding Them," *Washington Free Beacon*, June 6, 2025, freebeacon.com/campus/an-anti-american-propaganda-network-encouraged-violent-protests-at-columbia-then-produced-a-documentary-lauding-them/.

70. BreakThrough News, "How the Pro-Israel Lobby Hijacked Judaism and Spurred Trump's Crackdown," YouTube, video dated April 23, 2025, www.youtube.com/watch?v=p-2Aw2faQ24.

ism,"[71] while the latter, just one day after October 7, praised the attack and derisively mocked the "Israeli hipsters" who were murdered at the Supernova Music Festival.[72] *The Encampments* even includes an interview with Jamal Joseph, a Columbia professor and former Black Panther Party member who served time for manslaughter and harboring a fugitive, a detail omitted by the filmmakers.[73] These connections underscore how TPF's operations are deeply embedded within a network that aligns with Marxist ideologies and the Islamist agenda.

There are growing congressional concerns about TPF's financial ties and the organization's questionable involvement in disruptive behavior in American society. The Committee on Natural Resources, in December 2024, dispatched a letter to De Los Santos, addressing the organization's "unscrupulous financial ties" and "potentially improper political advocacy" following a violent protest in Washington, D.C., in July 2024.[74] The letter explicitly stated that the TPF "actively engages in disruptive demonstrations to support a pro-Hamas, anti-Israel agenda." Reports from the protest detailed demonstrators assaulting police officers, destroying federal property, burning and replacing American flags with foreign ones on federal property, and defacing the Columbus Plaza

---

71. Ben Becker, "Building a Real Left—Not One That Condemns Resistance and Is Without Palestinians," *Liberation*, December 18, 2023, liberationnews.org/building-a-real-left-not-one-that-condemns-resistance-and-has-no-palestinians/.

72. Brendan Gutenschwager, X, post dated October 8, 2023, x.com/BGOnTheScene/status/1711145162657673347.

73. Doreen St. Félix, "'The Encampments' and the American College Student," *New Yorker*, May 17, 2025, www.newyorker.com/culture/critics-notebook/the-encampments-and-the-american-college-student.

74. U.S. House of Representatives, "Letter to Manolos De Los Santos," U.S. House of Representatives—Committee on Natural Resources, December 9, 2024, naturalresources.house.gov/uploadedfiles/2024.12.05_hnr_the_peoples_forum_letter.pdf.

monument and the replica Liberty Bell with pro-Hamas graffiti. The ANSWER Coalition, which demonstrated alongside TPF, posted on social media in the month leading up to the event, listing the demonstration's collaborative partners, including CAIR and Code Pink, which I turn to next. The Committee on Natural Resources' letter further highlighted that TPF actively organizes alongside SJP and AMP, both of which have well-documented connections to Hamas, as discussed earlier in this chapter.

This network extends beyond TPF, as seen in its close coordination with another radical group—Code Pink—whose co-founder Jodie Evans is married to Singham, the financer who "calls the tunes" played by TPF. Code Pink positions itself as a women-led, peace organization devoted to "grassroots activism" and "social justice" causes, but its actions speak to a more nefarious plot. Code Pink frequently organizes protests with SJP and JVP and often co-opts the language of feminism and human rights, contributing to its positive image on the Left. On October 7, Code Pink offered no condemnation of Hamas' actions or condolences to the lives lost on that day. Instead, it blamed the conflict on the U.S. and Israel and defended Hamas's "resistance" to "occupation, colonization, and apartheid."[75]

In a critical demonstration of democratic oversight, U.S. lawmakers are addressing concerns regarding the relationship between Code Pink and the CCP. The House Committee on Natural Resources investigated the organization's potential ties to the Chinese government, referencing information that Code Pink works closely with the "Chinese media machine" and is part of a well-funded influence campaign by the CCP on American soil.[76] Nonprofit records highlighted by the committee re-

75. Code Pink, "CODEPINK Statement and the War in Palestine," Code Pink, October 8, 2023, www.codepink.org/occupation_is_indefensible.

76. House Committee on Natural Resources, "Committee Cracks Down on CCP Influence by Investigating Far-Left Nonprofit," House Committee on

vealed that, since 2017, about a quarter of Code Pink's donations—more than $1.4 million—have come from two groups linked to Singham. Code Pink's activism, as the House committee pointed out, demands that it register as a foreign agent in accordance with the Foreign Agents Registration Act (FARA), which requires individuals and organizations acting as agents of foreign governments to register with the Department of Justice. Senator Tom Cotton of Arkansas further accused Code Pink of being a front group of the CCP, adding, "It's no coincidence that the deranged [Code Pink] protesters who hate Israel also hate America."[77]

Code Pink's international links to the Leftist-Islamist alliance extend beyond China and into the Middle East. In September 2008, several Code Pink leaders met in New York City with Mahmoud Ahmadinejad, the former Iranian president who notoriously called for Israel to be wiped off the map, and later in the same year, met with Iranian government officials in Iran.[78] In the next year, Code Pink led a coalition of Leftist and Islamist activists to Gaza who were greeted by Ismail Haniyeh, then the leader of Hamas in Gaza, in a phone call.[79] These meetings reveal a practical application of the axiom "the enemy of my enemy is my friend." Their shared anti-American and anti-Israel sentiments form the foundation of the Leftist-Islamist alliance— an alliance based not

---

Natural Resources, November 16, 2023, naturalresources.house.gov/news/documentsingle.aspx?DocumentID=415189.

77. Israel National News, "Arkansas Senator Reacts to Disruption of Pete Hegseth's Senate Confirmation Hearing by the Anti-Israel Code Pink Group," *Israel National News*, January 14, 2025, www.israelnationalnews.com/news/402292.

78. Code Pink, "Official Release—CODEPINK Activists and Other Peace Organizations Meet with Iranian President in New York," Code Pink, September 24, 2008, www.codepink.org/official_release_codepink_activists_and_other_peace_organizations_meet_with_iranian_president_in_new_york.

79. Canary Mission, "Codepink," Canary Mission, n.d., canarymission.org/organization/CODEPINK.

on shared values per se but on a shared enemy.

The alliance is also theatrically on display in the European footprint of Code Pink. Though less omnipresent in Europe than in the United States, the group threw itself into the frenzy at the height of the Israel-Hamas war, endorsing and helping orchestrate some of London's largest marches, with crowds swelling past 500,000 under the "Together Alliance" banner. Activists were seen waving Palestinian flags and roaring against "genocide and fascism" while clogging central thoroughfares for hours. Code Pink coordinated direct-action campaigns targeting the U.K.-U.S. military bases on Cyprus, especially RAF Akrotiri, which served as a critical hub for intelligence gathering and surveillance flights for Israeli operations in Gaza. One particular high-profile Code Pink–led demonstration converged on London's Ministry of Defence itself, with activists blocking entrances and demanding Britain's immediate withdrawal from the Cyprus bases. Another solidarity rally materialized outside the British Embassy in Washington, D.C., where Code Pink and its allies rallied behind U.K.-based Palestine Action activists facing arrests and a government crackdown for their property-damaging raids on Israeli arms firms.

The enforcers of the Leftist-Islamist alliance—groups like The People's Forum and Code Pink—are more than willing to turn their weapons of social ostracism and professional destruction against any dissenter who dares to question their ideological purity. I know this from experience. I have personally been targeted for cancellation by the Leftist-Islamist alliance.

FROM COLLABORATION TO CANCELLATION: A SOCIOLOGICAL ACCOUNT OF ISLAMINSPANISH

The alliance's influence is not limited to large national organizations. Even smaller, seemingly benign groups can enforce ideological conformity, as I learned firsthand with IslamInSpanish, a Houston-based nonprofit dedicated to "educating Spanish-speaking individuals about Islam." Upon my arrival at Rice in 2015, I quickly established a rapport with the leaders of this organization, including founder and CEO Jaimie "Mujahid" Fletcher, his assistant Alex Gutierrez, and Imam Isa Parada, the group's director of education. All three leaders were Hispanic converts to Islam and, being close to my age, shared my familiarity with American culture, allowing for conversations spanning sports and pop culture to politics and religion. My interest in IslamInSpanish was sparked by the period of *la Convivencia*—the Spanish term for "coexistence"—in Islamic Spain. During the medieval period, tolerance flourished at times on the Iberian Peninsula, with Muslim administrations fostering religious, cultural, and academic freedom, at least relatively so for that point in history. That epoch, as I shared with a journalist for *Aramco World*, was a "golden era of science and medicine" where Jews, Christians, and Muslims lived in relative peace, with some Muslim leaders even embracing diversity in thought, philosophy, and scientific knowledge.[80]

IslamInSpanish's ability to cultivate *asabiya*, the Arabic term meaning "social cohesion," within its community, coupled with its expertise in utilizing media and technology to disseminate its message, struck me as noteworthy. I often saw the group as "pioneers" in its capacity to connect with diverse audiences through twenty-first-century technological advances. I applauded its work during my speech at the organization's National Latino Muslim convention and at several of its fundraising dinners. I also appeared in a Vice *Minority Reports* documentary about this organization, where I discussed the intersection of Islam, American

80. Joe Center, "Latino Muslims—Reclaiming a New World," *Aramco World*, September-October 2024, www.aramcoworld.com/articles/2024/september-october/latino-muslims---reclaiming-a-new-world.

identity, and Islamophobia.[81] My relationship with the group included hosting its leaders at Rice about a dozen times between 2015 and 2023. In 2019, they spoke to my "Muslims in American Society" course, an event that was featured by the *Houston Chronicle*.[82] Notably, the Middle East Forum, with which I am now affiliated, documented IslamInSpanish's visit in the "Campus Watch" section of its website, highlighting concerns about Islamism's integration into academia.[83] These activities and this past coverage remind me today of how easily well-intentioned individuals, particularly those navigating complex ideological landscapes like myself, can perform the "heavy lifting" for organizations that will swiftly abandon them the moment they deviate from prescribed ideological orthodoxy.

While IslamInSpanish engages in *dawah*, Arabic for "Islamic outreach," to inform audiences about Islam, critics claim that they are committed to proselytization and gaining converts to Islam. Initially, I did not perceive their efforts as overtly conversion-oriented, but my perspective shifted as I began to suspect they might be attempting to convert students and audiences to both Marxist worldviews and the Islamic faith.

The complexities of our relationship became apparent on October 12, 2023, just five days after October 7, when I hosted the group in my "Race and Ethnic Relations" class. The event, titled "Navigating Diversity in a Multicultural Community," veered at one point into a discussion of anti-colonialization and the idea that ethnic minorities, particularly

---

81. VICE, "Why Latinos Are Converting to Islam," YouTube, video dated January 17, 2019, www.youtube.com/watch?v=qOdu-lXCPFI.
82. Lindsay Peyton, "Rice Class Explores What It Means to Be Muslim in America," *Houston Chronicle*, December 5, 2019, www.houstonchronicle.com/lifestyle/houston-belief/article/Rice-class-explores-what-it-means-to-be-Muslim-in-14882186.php.
83. Alina Zhu, "Latinx Muslims Speak on Their Experiences in Sociology Class [incl. Craig Considine]," *Middle East Forum*, November 13, 2019, www.meforum.org/campus-watch/latinx-muslims-speak-on-their-experiences-in.

Hispanics, should shy away from adopting mainstream American values because it would be succumbing to "white hegemonic forces." While I would not call the conversation "anti-American," group members articulated a post-colonial narrative that portrayed the West negatively and positioned Islam as a source of "resistance" for ethnic minorities, which led to some underlying tension between members of the group and me. Even though Israel and Hamas were not explicitly discussed at this particular event, I sensed that IslamInSpanish leaned "pro-Palestinian," aligning with the "anti-colonial" framework often associated with Marxist thinking.

The simmering ideological tension between the group and me reached a breaking point during the student protests in the spring of 2024. My social media post condemning these protests, which subsequently led to significant challenges for me at Rice, caught the attention of IslamInSpanish's leadership. Alex Gutierrez, my usual contact for coordinating events with the group, informed me via text that they were severing ties due to my views and posts in support of Israel. He mentioned "local leadership" pressuring them to cancel our collaboration, raising questions about external influences, likely the group's donors, who might be dictating IslamInSpanish's affiliations. In looking back at this exchange, I also pause to question whether international players from the Leftist-Islamist alliance have sway over IslamInSpanish's operations. Fletcher, it is worth pointing out, spent five days in Qatar during the 2022 World Cup and published daily videos showing the "cultural richness" and "hospitality" of the Gulf nation, which, again, raises potential questions over which entities "pay" the IslamInSpanish "piper."[84]

The evolution of my relationship with IslamInSpanish underscores how post-colonial ideology, when adopted by this kind of organization or other explicitly Leftist groups, can lead to the "cancellation" of indi-

84. IslamInSpanishTV, "¿Hospitalidad en Carpas? Qatar 2022," YouTube, video dated December 13, 2022, www.youtube.com/watch?v=YVj59bLf9jI.

viduals who do not conform to ideological orthodoxy.

COUNTERING EXTREMIST ORGANIZATIONS: SHARAKA'S STAND FOR INTERFAITH CONNECTIONS

Not every organization in the civil sphere advances the Leftist-Islamist agenda. Some actively work to counter it. One such group is Sharaka, meaning "partnership" in Arabic, a nonprofit organization established in 2020 by Israelis, Emiratis, and Bahrainis.[85] Founded in the wake of the Abraham Accords, its purpose is to advance the vision of peace and cooperation by fostering people-to-people contact. This organization is actively working to shape a new Middle East, one built on cooperation, dialogue, friendship, and understanding, all of which stand as a direct antithesis to the divisive tactics employed by the groups analyzed earlier in this chapter. Those groups prioritize conflict over conciliation. Sharaka prioritizes the opposite.

Sharaka's unique strength lies in its diverse composition, including Israelis and Arabs, Jews, Muslims, Christians, and Druze from across the Middle East, all working together in the spirit of civility. By moving beyond biased narratives and divisive identity politics, Sharaka cultivates genuine understanding and fosters a path toward peace through "cultural immersion," directly undermining the tactics of the "foot soldiers" and their allies.

I had the opportunity to host the organization at Rice in February 2025, when several Sharaka team members presented a compelling case for a paradigm shift rooted in civic values and interfaith dialogue.[86] Alyssa

---

85. Sharaka, "Our Mission," Sharaka, n.d., www.sharakango.com/.

86. Craig Considine, "The Sharaka Effect—Transforming Campus Climates through Grassroots Diplomacy," *Jewish Herald-Voice*, February 27, 2025, jhvonline.com/the-sharaka-effect-transforming-campus-climates-through-grass-

Annis, a British Jew and Israeli citizen, shared her experience of feeling safer wearing her Star of David necklace in Morocco than in the United States, an indictment of the troubling rise of antisemitism in American society. Her views on Muslims took a turn when she joined a "death march" at Auschwitz, the ultimate symbol of Jewish suffering during the Holocaust, alongside Muslims from Abraham Accord countries. Her interactions with Arab Muslims in Morocco and Germany highlight the potential alliance for building solidarity in the most unexpected places and challenging the "oppressed" versus "oppressor" narrative promoted by the Leftist-Islamist alliance.

Errachid Montassir, a Muslim from rural Morocco, offered another compelling testament to Rice students regarding the transformative power of people-to-people contact. Growing up amidst deep-seated hatred towards Israelis and Jews, he initially perceived both as the embodiment of evil. However, a life-altering trip to Israel shattered his presumptions. He recounted a moving anecdote about his mother, who initially feared for his safety in Israel, but later recognized the trip's positive impact upon his return to Morocco. His story serves as a reminder to resist the allure of judging places and people from within rigid ideological bubbles, a core tenet of the Leftist-Islamist approach, which thrives on demonizing and isolating "the other," particularly Israelis and Jews.

Outside of a couple of hostile questions about the "atrocities" allegedly being conducted by Israel, the audience embraced the spirit of Sharaka's mission, and many Rice students were inspired by the group's courage, dedication, and honesty. The group's visit to campus shows the power of personal stories and heartfelt human connections and the importance of organizations combating the Leftist-Islamist agenda in the "soft war." For me personally, the experience was far more than just an exchange of ideas and stories. The event revealed the possibilities of con-

---

roots-diploma-p34586-113.htm.

structive people-to-people contact in the civil sphere.

In an era defined by ideological polarization and the weaponization of identity politics, organizations like Sharaka are not merely beneficial—they are indispensable. Supporting its efforts is crucial if we are to successfully challenge the narratives of confrontation and division. True solidarity, as Sharaka's work demonstrates, is built on empathy and mutual respect, not the cynical manipulation of "victimhood."

UNSEEN ARCHITECTS: THE NETWORKS PAVING THE WAY FOR POLITICAL POWER

This chapter has mapped the architecture of the Leftist-Islamist alliance—the funders, trainers, legal defenders, and propagandists who sustain the "soft war" in the civil sphere. These "knights" do not act in isolation. On the contrary, they coordinate with the pawns on campus and the bishops in the classroom. Their ultimate objective, however, is political power. The next chapter turns to the progressive politicians and lawmakers who translate this ideological infrastructure into concrete policy and legislation aimed at undermining the United States, Israel, and the broader West.

Chapter 4

The Political Front: The Progressive Conundrum and the Pushback from the Right

Having navigated the ideological convergence of students ("pawns"), professors ("bishops"), and organizations ("knights"), we now shift our focus to politicians ("rooks"). Unlike the subtle maneuvers of other pieces, politicians wield power through their direct ability to create or stifle legislation and to exert influence across the board. In this chapter, we examine how far-left progressive politicians, such as Rashida Tlaib, Ilhan Omar, Zohran Mamdani, and Alexandria Ocasio-Cortez, and third parties leverage their public platforms to "clear paths" for the Leftist-Islamist alliance. My argument is that modern progressivism, which often adopts a Marxist framework, is steering the West towards societal "regression" despite its claims of forward movement. A growing chorus of critics, including myself, contend that certain contemporary manifestations of "progression" deviate from traditional civic values such as civility, equality, and national pride and adopt a more authoritarian posture toward social change, which Orwell warned about. In

Europe, this same progressive movement has manifested in political parties and politicians that rely on Marxist-inspired ideas to champion Islamist demands.

RASHIDA TLAIB: THE "COMMANDER" IN THE HOUSE OF REPRESENTATIVES

As Sun Tzu observed in *The Art of War*, true mastery of the battlefield lies in defeating the enemy without direct military confrontation, a task often left to "commanders." From a strategic viewpoint, a commander is vested with the authority and responsibility to guide and lead forces at both tactical and strategic levels to achieve the mission's objectives. In this context, Rashida Tlaib, the Palestinian American progressive lawmaker and self-identified socialist, stands as such a commander for the Leftist-Islamist alliance in the House of Representatives. Her voting record and policy stances, such as supporting Hamas and calling for the abolition of ICE and the police, align with the alliance's agenda.

As I have done frequently throughout this book, I will share a relevant personal experience, which, in this instance, links my thesis to Tlaib. I spoke alongside her in February 2020, when I accepted an invitation from Muslims 4 Peace, a nonprofit organization based in New Jersey, to participate in an event at Rutgers University.[1] While the organization's website[2] advertised a mission of "interfaith activities" and "non-violence," its social media posts revealed an alignment with the Leftist-Islamist al-

1. Muslims 4 Peace, "A Global Crisis—Refugees, Migrants, and Asylum Seekers—Lessons from Prophet Muhammad (pbuh)," Muslims 4 Peace, n.d., muslims4peace.org/14th-annual-interfaith-prophet-muhammad-pbuh-conference/.

2. Muslims 4 Peace, "About Us," Muslims 4 Peace, n.d., muslims4peace.org/about-us/.

liance, including support for Mahmoud Khalil[3] and content supporting groups like Jewish Voice for Peace (JVP).[4] This contradiction highlights the deceptive nature of the alliance. Much like CAIR's presentation as a "civil rights advocacy group" rather than a Muslim Brotherhood front, Muslims 4 Peace presents a mask to conceal its true purpose.

Before the Rutgers panel, I attended a private fundraiser at the home of someone affiliated with Muslims 4 Peace. The basement setting, packed with fifty to sixty people, allowed individuals to mingle. My guide, another associate of Muslims 4 Peace, introduced me to two of Tlaib's staff members, both young Muslim American women, one of whom wore a hijab. With years of experience interacting in such environments, I immediately sensed that something was amiss. Tlaib's assistants were surprisingly cold and brisk, if not downright snarky, to me. This unexpected chill surprised me, especially considering my writing and advocacy at that time focused on countering "Islamophobia." Shortly thereafter, my guide introduced me to Tlaib herself, who appeared to double down on the "cold shoulder." Her handshake was quick and unserious, and she avoided eye contact. It felt as though she and her team had pre-planned this dismissive treatment. I left the fundraiser a bit confused, having assumed Tlaib's team and I were on the "same page." Apparently not.

My exchange with her led me to wonder if her team's discomfort stemmed from my interfaith advocacy for the United Arab Emirates, a country that is frequently criticized by Muslim Brotherhood entities for normalizing relations with Israel, which later manifested in the Abraham Accords. As I have mentioned, the Abraham Accords are "kryptonite" for the Leftist-Islamist alliance, as they sidestepped Hamas's mil-

---

3. Muslims 4 Peace, "Facebook Post," Muslims 4 Peace, March 12, 2024, www.facebook.com/share/p/1CKPbre1Xz/.

4. Muslims 4 Peace, Facebook, post dated December 31, 2024, www.facebook.com/share/p/1AgozjD59F/.

itaristic "resistance" in favor of peace between Israel and its neighboring Arab states.

The actual conference itself was not without its tensions, with "anti-Palestinian" and "anti-Zionist" demonstrations both supporting and opposing the event. During Tlaib's speech, a protester—Dov Hikind, a Jewish Zionism activist and former Democrat who once served in the New York State Assembly—interrupted Tlaib and challenged her history of antisemitic statements. Hikind was promptly removed by a young man in a Palestinian *keffiyeh*, a headdress that serves as a symbol of Palestinian "resistance," with Rutgers police supporting the removal as the crowd cheered in Tlaib's defense.[5] It appeared as if the "system" at Rutgers, at least the "institutional structure" put in place that day, fully supported Tlaib, a reality reminiscent of the institutional support seen for the "foot soldiers" on university campuses across the country.

As rooks on the metaphorical chessboard, progressive politicians in Congress do far more than provide speeches in front of conferences, rallies, and protests. Their power to vote and dictate law is paramount in realizing the Leftist-Islamist agenda. Just weeks after October 7, 2023, Tlaib voted "no" on a House resolution supporting Israel and condemning Hamas.[6] She was one of only nine representatives to do so. When questioned about her "no" vote, Tlaib claimed, "Israel is an apartheid state," a common and widely believed antisemitic charge made by those who are part of the alliance.[7] Less than a month later, Tlaib took to social

---

5. Gary Fouse, "Dov Hikind Thrown Out of Rashida Tlaib Event at Rutgers [incl. Craig Considine]," *Middle East Forum*, February 10, 2020, www.meforum.org/campus-watch/dov-hikind-thrown-out-of-rashid-tlaib-event.

6. Olafimihan Oshin, "These 9 Democrats Voted Against Resolution Backing Israel, Condemning Hamas," *The Hill*, October 25, 2023, thehill.com/homenews/house/4276005-these-democrats-voted-against-resolution-backing-israel/.

7. Ibid.

media, posting that "From the river to the sea"—a slogan that makes an inherent demand for the eradication of Israel—is an "aspirational call for freedom, human rights, and peaceful coexistence," rather than a genocidal call to wipe out the world's only Jewish state.[8] She stood by her comments and strategically reframed the narrative by accusing her colleagues, who claimed her statements were antisemitic, of "silencing" her. These actions and statements reveal an Orwellian narrative of manipulation, where reality is inverted to serve a specific political agenda, and a Marxist narrative of "oppression," where any kind of opposition to one's remarks is branded "discrimination" based on identity politics.

Similar support for Hamas is found among European politicians. Jean-Luc Mélenchon, leader of La France Insoumise (LFI), a far-left French party, refused to describe the October 7 Hamas attacks as terrorism, calling them an "armed offensive" instead.[9] The LFI has been rightfully accused of fostering an "Islamo-leftist" alliance with strong pro-Hamas activism and sympathies. Similarly, in the British context, Jeremy Corbyn, the former Labour Party leader, has a deep history of pro-Hamas and pro-Hezbollah sympathies, once even calling members of both organizations "friends."[10] Hamas has praised him for his support at pro-Palestinian rallies around the United Kingdom. Corbyn, like Mélenchon, consistently frames Israel's actions as "apartheid" and "genocide." Bottom line, the pattern in the United States is not unique, as sim-

8. Ken Coleman, "Tlaib Stands by Her Defense of Palestinian Slogan, 'From the River to the Sea,'" *Michigan Advance*, November 6, 2023, michiganadvance.com/2023/11/06/tlaib-stands-by-her-defense-of-pro-palestinanian-slogan-from-the-river-to-the-sea/.

9. Christophe Ayad, "Mélenchon Accused of Glorifying Terrorism after Remarks about October 7," *Le Monde*, July 1, 2026, www.lemonde.fr/en/france/article/2026/07/01/melenchon-accused-of-glorifying-terrorism-after-remarks-about-october-7_6755037_7.html.

10. "Jeremy Corbyn Refuses to Condemn Hamas 'Friends,'" *Jerusalem Post*, October 9, 2023, www.jpost.com/international/article-765302.

ilar alliances among European politicians platform Hamas sympathizers under the guise of "anti-imperialism."

Tlaib's maneuvers in Congress are consistently bolstered by the organizations and networks operating on behalf of the Leftist-Islamist alliance in the civil sphere. CAIR, for instance, has issued countless press releases—too numerous to detail here—either calling for supporting Tlaib's resolutions or defending her against accusations of antisemitism. In May 2025, CAIR urged the House to support House Resolution 409, introduced by Tlaib, which recognized the Palestinian *nakba*, or "catastrophe" in Arabic.[11] This resolution refers to the period between 1947 and 1949, during which Palestinians were, according to CAIR, "forcibly displaced" in an act of "mass expulsion" and "ethnic cleansing" initiated by the newly created state of Israel. Crucially, CAIR's press release omitted any discussion of the war of extermination launched by Arab countries against Jews and the young state of Israel.

The Israeli counterargument maintains that the 1948 war between Israeli and Arab countries was a defensive response to an existential threat, as Arab states rejected the United Nations participation plan that Jews accepted.[12] Subsequently, the Arab states neighboring Israel launched a coordinated invasion, with leaders like Azzam Pasha, the Secretary-General of the Arab League, declaring it a "war of extermination and momentous massacre."[13] The Jerusalem Center for Security and

11. Council on American-Islamic Relations, "CAIR Action Alert—Urge Congress to Support Rep. Tlaib's Resolution Recognizing 77th Anniversary of Nakba, Affirming Palestinian Rights," Council on American-Islamic Relations, May 16, 2025, www.cair.com/press_releases/cair-action-alert-urge-congress-to-support-rep-tlaibs-resolution-recognizing-77th-anniversary-of-nakba-affirming-palestinian-rights/.

12. Matthias Küntzel, "The 1948 Arab War Against Israel: An Aftershock of World War II?," *Fathom Journal*, Autumn 2015, fathomjournal.org/the-1948-arab-war-against-israel-an-aftershock-of-world-war-ii/.

13. Efraim Karsh, "Azzam's Genocidal Threat," *Middle East Quarterly* 19,

Foreign Affairs precisely summarized the dynamics during this period, offering an important counter-narrative:

> The defeat of [the Arab] armies and their political failure in opposing the partition of Mandatory Palestine are thus rewritten [by the likes of Tlaib], with the [*nakba*], as a shocking, congenital injustice of which they are victims. This injustice is affixed to the very existence of Israel, which, in order to exist, purportedly dispossessed an innocent people from their land so that it could take their place. The Palestinian aggressors became the victims. The extermination of others became self-pity and compassion.[14]

CAIR's omission highlights a key strategy in the "soft war" we have been discussing—narratives are carefully curated, and the truth is twisted to serve a political objective. In this case, the *nakba* has been "repositioned," in a clear Gramscian, counter-hegemony-style maneuver, to frame Palestinians as the "perpetual victims." This strategic reframing by Tlaib carries symbolism in its attempt to "control the narrative," much like the Inner Party's "Ministry of Truth" that Orwell wrote about in *Nineteen Eighty-Four*. The "Ministry of Truth," over time, rewrote historical records and altered facts to erase "inconvenient truths." This assisted the Inner Party in achieving its goal—to always align the past with the party's current ideological agenda.

Tlaib and CAIR's strategic reframing of history is reinforced by Tlaib's ideological connections to Marxist groups advocating for communism and Fanonian liberation movements. One illustration of her alignment occurred in April 2025, when she addressed the annual conference

---

no. 2 (2012): 27–36, www.meforum.org/middle-east-quarterly/azzam-genocide-threat.

14. Shmuel Trigano, "Deconstructing the Three Stages of the Nakba Myth," Jerusalem Center for Security and Foreign Affairs, November 10, 2019, jcpa.org/article/deconstructing-the-three-stages-of-the-nakba-myth/.

of the Palestinian American Community Center (PACC) in Clifton, New Jersey.[15] The PACC, a registered 501(c)(3) nonprofit organization, describes itself as "a non-political and non-religious organization" whose mission is to "empower" the Palestinian community.[16] A glimpse into its official 2025 statements, however, reveals a different story, with titles advocating for the world to "rise for justice," a Marxist revolutionary call, and memorializing the "ongoing genocide" in Palestine.[17] Sharing the PACC platform with Tlaib was Wisam Rafeedie, a prominent leader of the Popular Front for the Liberation of Palestine (PFLP), the Marxist Palestinian terrorist organization founded in 1967 and designated a "terrorist entity" by the U.S. government in October 1997. The conference's promotional materials featured logos and paraphernalia of Samidoun, the nongovernmental organization jointly designated a "terrorist entity" by both the U.S. and Canadian governments in October 2024.[18] In its official designation, the U.S. government described Samidoun as a "sham charity" that serves as one of PFLP's international financiers and masquerades as a charity claiming to provide "humanitarian support" to those in need.[19] But as the Department of the Treasury noted, this organization "diverts funds for much-needed assistance to support terrorist groups."[20]

---

15. NGO Monitor, "NGO Ties to Terror-linked New Jersey Conference Featuring Rashida Tlaib and PFLP Member," *NGO Monitor*, April 6, 2025, ngo-monitor.org/reports/ngo-ties-to-terror-linked-new-jersey-conference-featuring-rashida-tlaib-and-pflp-member/.

16. Palestinian American Community Center, "Who We Are!", Palestinian American Community Center, n.d., www.paccusa.org/about-us.html.

17. Ibid.

18. U.S. Department of the Treasury, "United States and Canada Target Key International Fundraiser for Foreign Terrorist Organization," press release, October 15, 2024, home.treasury.gov/news/press-releases/jy2646.

19. Ibid.

20. Ibid.

Yet, the organization continues to operate freely in the United States through a network of agents, shell organizations, and newly created proxy groups, raising concerning questions about the effectiveness of the government's counterterrorism strategies.[21] Comparatively, Germany banned Samidoun activities in 2023,[22] and dissolved the subgroup Samidoun Deutschland, citing their support for Hamas, antisemitic propaganda, and spontaneous "celebrations" in the wake of October 7, while the Dutch Parliament voted to designate the group as a "terrorist" organization in 2024.[23] Belgium and Sweden, both of which have highly active Samidoun chapters, would be wise to follow their European counterparts' maneuver in the "soft war" against Islamist entities in Europe.

Another key point to highlight with PFLP and Samidoun is that both groups have been linked to the Palestinian Youth Movement (PYM), which Influence Watch describes as "an anti-Israel activist group made up of Palestinian youths who believe they are kept from their homeland by Israel."[24] Senator Tom Cotton called for the Internal Revenue Service to investigate the PYM for allegedly violating American tax laws, citing its links to the PFLP, Samidoun, and other groups like SJP.[25] The PYM is fiscally sponsored by Westchester People's Ac-

---

21. Michael Starr, "Same Network, New Names—Terror Front Samidoun Secretly Operates in US, Canada Via Proxies Post-Ban," *Jerusalem Post*, September 4, 2025, www.jpost.com/diaspora/antisemitism/article-866373.
22. Federal Ministry of the Interior and Community (BMI), "HAMAS and Samidoun Banned in Germany," press release, November 2, 2023, www.bmi.bund.de/SharedDocs/pressemitteilungen/EN/2023/11/banned-hamas-samidoun.html.
23. "Netherlands to Add Samidoun to List of Terrorist Groups," *Jerusalem Post*, October 12, 2024, www.jpost.com/diaspora/article-824116#google_vignette.
24. Influence Watch, "Palestinian Youth Movement USA," Influence Watch, n.d., www.influencewatch.org/non-profit/palestinian-youth-movement-usa/.
25. Tom Cotton, "Letter to the Honorable Scott Bessent," United States Senate, August 22, 2025, www.cotton.senate.gov/imo/media/doc/82225cotton-

tion Coalition (Wespac), a group that supports a variety of anti-Israel initiatives.[26] Samidoun and PYM's joint strategy of operating without direct confrontation in the military realm allows Tlaib to subtly advance their agenda and leverage their network, which seemingly includes her, to provide "ammunition" for the Leftist-Islamist cause.

As a "commander" of the Leftist-Islamist alliance, Tlaib inevitably faces significant pressure as she maneuvers about the "soft war" landscape. When a commander is distressed, a "lieutenant," the next rank in command, often steps in to provide moral support and reinforce resolve. We saw this dynamic unfold in November 2023, when Tlaib delivered a speech on the House floor in which she emotionally stated, with a crack in her voice, "I can't believe I have to say this, but Palestinian people are not disposable."[27] As she paused to regain her composure, Ilhan Omar, another progressive in the House of Representatives, rose and put a supportive hand on Tlaib's back. Tlaib continued, "What I don't understand is why the cries of Palestinians sound different to you all."[28] Her pivot—deflecting from Hamas's actions on October 7 to condemning Israel—exemplifies "whataboutism," a tactic attributed to communist regimes whereby individuals neutralize a critique of one side by redirecting blame entirely onto the other. In addition to reinforcing the "oppressed" versus "oppressor" binary, Tlaib failed to condemn or even acknowledge Hamas's oppression of Palestinians. Predictably, she drew intense opposition from her colleagues in the House, a place where advocating for

---

pymletter.pdf.

26. Influence Watch, "Palestinian Youth Movement USA," Influence Watch, n.d.

27. Emily Atkinson, "Rashida Tlaib Censured over Israel-Gaza Comments," *BBC News*, November 8, 2023, www.bbc.com/news/world-us-canada-67354706.

28. Jacob Fischler, "U.S. House Votes to Censure Michigan's Rashida Tlaib over Israel Remarks," *Louisiana Illuminator*, November 7, 2023, lailluminator.com/2023/11/07/tlaib-censure/.

terrorist groups carries immense weight. Nonetheless, she maintained support from her fellow "comrades," particularly Omar. In this way, Tlaib and Omar operate as interlocking rooks, combining narrative control with legislative votes to advance the cause of both Leftism and Islamism.

ILHAN OMAR: FROM REFUGEE TO PROGRESSIVE ISLAMIST

If Tlaib is a "commander" of the Leftist-Islamist alliance, then Ilhan Omar is a "lieutenant." In military terms, a lieutenant is primarily tasked with strategy at the tactical level, focusing on training soldiers and executing plans relating to certain missions. This tactical focus finds a parallel in Omar's formative experiences and her subsequent political trajectory. Her early life was shaped by displacement and the search for refuge. Born in Mogadishu, Somalia, her family fled the Somali civil war in 1991, subsequently spending four years in the Utange refugee camp near Mombasa, Kenya. In 1995, at the age of twelve, she and her family immigrated to the U.S. as refugees, initially settling in Arlington, Virginia, before relocating to Minneapolis, Minnesota. She became a U.S. citizen in 2000, at the age of seventeen.

Since entering the House of Representatives in 2018, Omar has become a controversial figure, in large part due to her statements about the United States, the country that welcomed her as a refugee. In 2025, she stated that the United States is "turning into one of the worst countries on earth,"[29] a sweeping, if not ludicrous, condemnation that echoes Said's Orientalist critique by inverting the narrative so that the West itself becomes the "backward" force in relation to the "Orient." In 2021,

29. Grabien Staff, "Rep. Ilhan Omar Says the U.S. Is Becoming Worse Than Her Home Country of Somalia," *Grabienews*, July 17, 2025, news.grabien.com/story/rep-ilhan-omar-says-the-us-is-becoming-worse-than-her-home-country-of.

she compared America and Israel to Hamas and the Taliban,[30] making an egregious moral equivalency between democratic countries and authoritarian regimes that deploys Orwellian doublethink to erase any meaningful distinction between liberal democracies like the United States and terrorist organizations like Hamas and the Taliban. A year earlier, she stated, "We are not merely fighting to tear down the systems of oppression in the criminal justice system. We are fighting to tear down systems of oppression that exist in housing, in education, in health care, in employment, in the air we breathe,"[31] a statement that clearly reveals Gramsci's strategy of cultural hegemony, whereby the West's existing structures and civil society should be dismantled to usher in the new revolutionary order. In an earlier 2018 interview with *Al Jazeera*, Omar said that Americans should be "fearful" of white men and that the country "should be profiling, monitoring, and creating policies to fight the radicalization of White men." Here, once again we see the logic of the CRT paradigm, in which "whiteness" is an ultimate evil to be defeated in American society.[32]

These kinds of statements have been the subject of a Republican-led House Resolution accusing her of advocating "for a Marxist form of government that is incompatible with the principles laid out in the

30. BBC News, "Ilhan Omar—US Congresswoman Defends 'Offensive' Israel Remark," *BBC News*, June 10, 2021, www.bbc.com/news/world-us-canada-57436573.

31. Adam Shaw, "House GOP Resolution Accuses Ilhan Omar of 'Anti-American' Remarks; Office Decries 'False Smear,'" *Fox News*, July 16, 2020, www.foxnews.com/politics/house-gop-resolution-accuses-ilhan-omar-of-anti-american-remarks-marxist-policies

32. "US Should Be More Fearful of White Men, Says Ilhan Omar in Resurfaced Clip Shared by Laura Loomer," *Times of India*, May 5, 2025, timesofindia.indiatimes.com/world/us/us-should-be-more-fearful-of-white-men-says-ilhan-omar-in-resurfaced-clip-shared-by-laura-loomer/articleshow/120894021.cms.

founding documents of the United States."[33] Even Omar's Democratic colleagues have criticized her, calling her equation of the United States and Israel with Hamas and the Taliban "as offensive as it is misguided," adding, "Ignoring the differences between democracies governed by the rule of law and contemptible organizations that engage in terrorism at best discredits one's intended argument and at worst reflects deep-seated prejudice."[34] Unsurprisingly, Omar responded, like Tlaib, by playing the "victim" and resorting to her defense that her fellow Democrats were using "Islamophobic tropes" and attempting to "silence" her. In doing so, she again exemplified Orwell by manipulating language, delegitimizing criticism, and making dissent impossible, all to ensure that the Left-ist-Islamist alliance's "truth" is the only acceptable one.

Omar's tenure in Congress is further marked by her antisemitic views, which are apparent in her statements about Jewish people and capitalism. She has accused her colleagues of being "bought" by Israel and claimed that America's political system is controlled by Jewish campaign donations from lobbying groups like the bipartisan American Israel Public Affairs Committee (AIPAC). This sentiment, where financial influence is portrayed as controlling political allegiance, sheds light on historical tropes rooted in Marxist ideology. Marx himself, in his essay "On the Jewish Question," conflated Jewish people with capitalism and finance, reducing them and their faith to a "capitalist function" and portraying their "economic influence" as destructive. Omar built on this Marxist position in February 2019, when she ignited a firestorm by posting to social media the words, "It's all about the Benjamins, baby"—sug-

33. Shaw, "House GOP Resolution Accuses Ilhan Omar of 'Anti-American' Remarks; Office Decries 'False Smear.'"

34. Brad Schneider, "Statement on Congresswoman Omar Equating the United States and Israel to Hamas and the Taliban," press statement, June 9, 2021, schneider.house.gov/media/press-releases/statement-congresswoman-omar-equating-united-states-and-israel-hamas-and.

gesting that U.S. politicians are controlled by Jewish Americans and Israel.[35] (The term "Benjamin" refers to a $100 bill, which features the face of Benjamin Franklin.) This quote encapsulates both the anti-capitalist and anti-Jewish rhetoric driving the Leftist-Islamist alliance, which weaves together Marxist narratives to reframe Jewish Americans and the pro-Israel lobby as the invisible hand controlling the U.S. government.

Omar's activities also reveal ties to Muslim Brotherhood–affiliated organizations.[36] These concerns extend to her participation in public events, such as a 2019 panel discussion with Islamic Relief, a prominent Islamic charitable organization founded in 1984 that House representatives called to be investigated by the IRS and FBI in 2018.[37] Islamic Relief has drawn significant international scrutiny, with the U.A.E. designating its headquarters as a "terrorist organization"[38] and Hongkong and Shanghai Banking Corporation (HSBC) closing its bank accounts.[39] Like Tlaib, Omar also works with CAIR in the civil sphere. Speaking at the organization's fundraiser in March 2019, she talked about the "oppression" of Muslim Americans, the impact of "Western imperialism," and CAIR's "noble" founding. She also claimed that Muslim Americans

35. John Bresnahan, "Ilhan Omar Ignites New Anti-Semitism Controversy with Comments on AIPAC," *Politico*, February 10, 2019, www.politico.com/story/2019/02/10/ilhan-omar-israel-aipac-money-1163631.

36. Bradley Martin, "Muslim Reform Groups Praise Rep. Ilhan Omar's Ouster," *Jerusalem News Syndicate*, February 20, 2023, www.jns.org/muslim-reform-groups-praise-rep-ilhan-omars-ouster/.

37. Middle East Forum, "MEF Reveals Islamic Relief under Investigation; Congress Demands Answers," *Middle East Forum*, October 18, 2018, www.meforum.org/mef-reveals-islamic-relief-under-investigation.

38. Emirati News Agency, "UAE Cabinet Approves List of Designated Terrorist Organisations, Groups," *Emirati News Agency*, November 15, 2014, www.wam.ae/en/details/1395272478814.

39. Shafik Mandhai, "HSBC Bank Cuts Off Services to Muslim Sharity," *Al Jazeera*, January 4, 2016, www.aljazeera.com/economy/2016/1/4/hsbc-bank-cuts-off-services-to-muslim-charity.

were "second-class citizens," encouraged her followers to be "tired" of this alleged position, called on the audience to "raise hell," and motivated attendees to "make people uncomfortable," all subtle cries of "rebellion" and "resistance" that Marx and Fanon would endorse.[40]

The role of Omar within the Leftist-Islamist alliance precedes her anti-American and antisemitic positions as a House representative. In 2017, as a Minnesota state representative, she met with Recep Tayyip Erdoğan, the Islamist president of Turkey and key ally of the Muslim Brotherhood, in a meeting facilitated by CAIR.[41] Two years later, Omar would face criticism as a member of Congress after voting "present" on House Resolution 296, which formally recognized the mass killings of Armenians by Ottoman Turks in 1915 and 1916 as "genocide."[42] The resolution passed the House by an overwhelming 405-to-11 margin. Omar responded to criticism of her "present" (effectively a "no") vote by criticizing the United States, claiming that the American government "should be committed to addressing genocide and other atrocity crimes without needing a political reason to drive it." Leaders of the Armenian American community denounced Omar for parroting the Turkish government's talking points. The Armenian Council of America, a California-based group, similarly accused her of using "official genocide denialist rhetoric," a phrasing with Orwellian implications in that a politician denied reality and used manipulative language to craft a new narrative to

---

40. Valerie Richardson, "Ilhan Omar at CAIR Speech Tells Muslims to 'Raise Hell,'" *Washington Times*, March 24, 2019, www.washingtontimes.com/news/2019/mar/24/ilhan-omar-ciar-speech-tells-muslims-raise-hell/.

41. Dalia Al-Aqidi, "Ilhan Omar and Her Fascination with Radical Islamists," *Arab News*, November 27, 2022, www.arabnews.com/node/2207061.

42. Daniel Arkin, "Ilhan Omar Faces Blowback after Voting 'Present' on Armenian Genocide," *NBC News*, October 30, 2019, www.nbcnews.com/news/us-news/ilhan-omar-faces-blowback-after-voting-present-armenian-genocide-resolution-n1073991.

fulfill an ideological purpose.[43] These kinds of maneuvers on the international front led to a 2023 House vote that removed Omar from her position on the Foreign Affairs Committee.[44] She responded by resorting to CRT, claiming that her removal was "politically motivated" by other House members who do not believe an African Muslim refugee should serve in Congress.[45]

Omar's strategic impact within the Leftist-Islamist alliance extends to her direct support to the "foot soldiers." In April 2024, Omar and her daughter, Isra Hirsi, appeared at an anti-Israel encampment at Columbia University.[46] There, Omar decried Israel's "genocide" of the Palestinians and argued that the student encampments were being "co-opted and made to look bad" by politicians and members of the media.[47] In this instance, Omar employed tactics reminiscent of several key theorists discussed in this book. She drew on Orwell's focus on "narratives" and how they can be used to manipulate reality, simultaneously accusing the opposition of the very act she herself is guilty of—controlling public consciousness by reframing discourse around the loaded term "genocide." Absent from her remarks was any mention of Hamas's genocidal acts on October 7, or indeed, any reference to the historical genocide of the Holocaust. Instead, she accused Israel of committing genocide and condemned Columbia for allegedly serving as an Israeli ally. Republicans in the House of Representatives responded to Omar's comments

43. Ibid.

44. Kayla Epstein, "Republicans Oust Ilhan Omar from Powerful House Committee," *BBC News*, February 2, 2023, www.bbc.com/news/world-us-canada-64493018.

45. Martin, "Muslim Reform Groups Praise Rep. Ilhan Omar's Ouster."

46. Kyle Morris, "Ilhan Omar, Daughter Appear at Columbia University Encampment amid Nationwide Anti-Israel Protests," *Fox News*, April 25, 2024, www.foxnews.com/politics/ilhan-omar-daughter-appear-columbia-university-encampment-amid-nationwide-anti-israel-protests.

47. Ibid.

at the encampment by issuing House Resolution 1207, which censured her for her history of antisemitism.[48] According to the resolution, Omar referred to Jewish students at Columbia as "pro-genocide." These reverse accusations of genocide against Israel have functioned as a rhetorical shield to deflect recognition of Hamas's own genocidal actions.[49]

Isra Hirsi, a "foot soldier" who was arrested and issued a summons for trespassing on Columbia's campus by the NYPD, was later suspended from Barnard College, a branch of Columbia, for illegal activities in campus demonstrations.[50] She, in turn, claimed the suspension was for "standing in solidarity with Palestinians facing a genocide," a quote that reflects a dominant trend within the progressive movement—a tendency to invoke "institutional discrimination" and utilize identity politics rather than upholding proper civil decorum, defending the law in the public sphere, and standing for accountability for one's actions.[51] In another part of her statement, Omar's daughter said that she would "stand resolute until our demands are met," which included advancing BDS-aligned strategies and providing amnesty for "all students facing repression."[52]

---

48. "Censuring Representative Ilhan Omar of Minnesota for Her Recent Hateful Comments and History of Antisemitism," Congressional Bills 118th Congress, House Resolution 1207 introduced on May 7, 2024, www.congress.gov/118/bills/hres1207/BILLS-118hres1207ih.htm.
49. Avraham Russell Shalev, "Hamas' October 7th Genocide—Legal Analysis and the Weaponisation of Reverse Accusations—A Study in Modern Genocide Recognition and Denial," *Israel Law Review*, www.cambridge.org/core/journals/israel-law-review/article/hamas-october-7th-genocide-legal-analysis-and-the-weaponisation-of-reverse-accusations-a-study-in-modern-genocide-recognition-and-denial/322198E636341BE82F37ED7147FEB0F5.
50. Louis Casiano, "Rep. Ilhan Omar's Daughter Arrested and Released amid NYC Anti-Israel Protests at Columbia University," *Fox News*, April 18, 2024, www.foxnews.com/us/rep-ilhan-omars-daughter-custody-amid-nyc-anti-israel-protests-columbia-university.
51. Ibid.
52. Ibid.

Here, Omar's daughter again resorted to "repression" instead of framing her activities as those that were illegal according to legal boundaries.

Another revealing case involving Isra Hirsi occurred when she publicly supported Mohsen Mahdawi, a Columbia student activist whose green card was revoked and who faced deportation over his support for Hamas. Omar's daughter supported a fundraiser for Mahdawi that framed him as an "advocate for peace and justice," despite his repeated expressions of support for Hamas, a "narrative strategy" akin to CAIR framing itself solely as a "civil rights advocacy organization."[53] The record shows that at one Columbia protest, Mahdawi declared that there is "nothing more honorable than dying for a noble cause," a quote signaling his willingness to embrace "martyrdom" for Hamas's "revolution."[54] According to the *Washington Free Beacon*, his advocacy for "martyrdom" may be linked to his familial background, as Mahdawi once posted pictures to his Instagram account honoring the "martyrdom" of his "cousin," Maysara Masharqa, who served as a prominent field commander in the military wing of the Al-Aqsa Martyrs Brigade,[55] a U.S.-government designated terror group that participated in the October 7 attack alongside Hamas.[56] More seriously than mere rhetoric, court records allege that "Mahdawi told a gun shop owner that he used firearms to 'kill Jews'" while he was in Palestine.[57] According to the Department of Home-

53. Jessica Costescu, "Ilhan Omar's Daughter Fundraises for Columbia Activist in ICE Custody Who Endorsed Oct. 8 Attack," *Washington Free Beacon*, April 16, 2025, freebeacon.com/campus/ilhan-omars-daughter-fundraises-for-columbia-activist-in-ice-custody-who-endorsed-oct-7-attack/.

54. Ibid.

55. Ibid.

56. Ibid.

57. U.S. Department of Homeland Security, "The Real Story: DHS Sets the Record Straight on Terrorist Sympathizer and Leader of the Columbia Pro-Terrorist Riots Mohsen Mahdawi," May 9, 2025, www.dhs.gov/news/2025/05/09/real-story-dhs-sets-record-straight-terrorist-sympathizer-and-leader-colum-

land Security, the court records also noted a concerned individual who reported that Mahdawi claimed to have a history of making guns for Hezbollah.

As we have observed in the case of Omar and her daughter, radicalization is often a "family affair" in that parents are able to radicalize their children quite easily. Omar has not only publicly condoned her daughter's activities but also applauded her for her "courage and compassion" and for "stepping up to change what [she] cannot tolerate."[58] This dynamic highlights a recurring pattern whereby influential progressive leaders, much like Zohran Mamdani, whom I turn to next, are often shaped in their formative and collegiate years by certain ideologies present in familial environments.

THE STANDARD-BEARER: ZOHRAN MAMDANI'S "CHAMPAGNE SOCIALISM"

If Tlaib serves as a "commander" and Omar as a "lieutenant," then Zohran Mamdani, the New York City socialist mayor, stands as a "standard bearer" for the alliance. This military term evokes the image of one who carries the flag or standard, visibly representing the cause and leading the "foot soldiers" into ideological battle, a "rook" type role that Mamdani has embraced with notable fervor. His rise to prominence, following his victory in New York City's mayoral race, is anchored in a narrative of being part of a "marginalized" community, yet he comes from an "elite" background, which, according to Marxist theory, ironically makes him an "oppressor." His mother, Mira Nair, is an Oscar-nominated director and Hollywood filmmaker who has received significant financial sup-

bia-pro.

58. Morris, "Ilhan Omar, Daughter Appear at Columbia University Encampment amid Nationwide Anti-Israel Protests."

port from Qatar,[59] while his father, Mahmood Mamdani, holds a distinguished position as a Columbia University professor specializing in the Fanonian liberation movements.[60] Upon their move from Uganda to New York City, the Mamdani family enrolled their son in the Bank Street School for Children, a private Upper West Side PK–8 school that promises a "progressive approach" to education and charges nearly seventy thousand dollars per year for tuition, and later the Bronx High School of Science,[61] an acclaimed institution recognized as the fourth-best high school in New York City and the thirty-seventh best in America.[62] To further underscore his "elite" upbringing, the Mamdani family celebrated Zohran's wedding in July 2025 with a "lavish, three-day affair" at his family's "ritzy" and "secluded" Ugandan compound, complete with "masked security guards" and a "cellphone jamming system."[63]

This elitism, coupled with Mamdani's critique of capitalism and advocacy for socialism, reveals the archetype of a "champagne socialist," a

---

59. Hannah Brown, "Mamdani's Mother Collected Millions in Qatari Cash, Raising Foreign Influence Concerns—NYP," *Jerusalem Post*, September 5, 2025, www.jpost.com/american-politics/article-866430.
60. Matthew Haag and Emma Goldberg, "The Parents Who Helped Shape Zohran Mamdani's Politics," *New York Times*, June 26, 2025, www.nytimes.com/2025/06/26/nyregion/zohran-mamdani-parents-mira-nair.html.
61. Megan Sauer, "Zohran Mamdani Ran for VP of His High School and Lost —Now He's Winning the Democratic Primary for NYC mayor," *CNBC*, June 27, 2025, www.cnbc.com/2025/06/27/zohran-mamdanis-political-career-started-in-high-school.html.
62. U.S. News and World Report, "Bronx High School of Science," *U.S. News and World Report*, n.d., www.usnews.com/education/best-high-schools/new-york/districts/new-york-city-public-schools/bronx-high-school-of-science-13207.
63. Emma Bussey, "Inside Socialist Zohran Mamdani's Posh Wedding Bash at Secluded Uganda Compound—Complete with Phone Jamming System, Armed Guards," *New York Post*, July 26, 2025, nypost.com/2025/07/26/us-news/zohran-mamdanis-presidential-style-uganda-wedding-bash/.

term denoting an individual who champions socialist ideals to assist the "oppressed," while simultaneously enjoying a life of considerable luxury and privilege. Orwell warned about "champagne socialists" with his depiction of the pigs in *Animal Farm*. The pigs initially lead the revolution against human oppression under the slogan of "All animals are equal," but over time, Napoleon, the leader of the pigs, and his chief propagandist, Squealer, consolidate power and corrupt the system to acquire more privileges for themselves. As the plot of *Animal Farm* thickens, the pigs move into the farmhouse previously inhabited by humans, sleep in beds, and wear clothes, all while the other animals toil and suffer.

Mamdani's familial background and academic pursuits, including co-founding a branch of SJP in 2013 at Bowdoin College, cement his alignment with the foundational tenets of the Leftist-Islamist alliance.[64] Two years before founding Bowdoin-SJP, his father, Mahmood, delivered the keynote address at the inaugural SJP national conference in October 2011. In his speech, Mamdani Senior drew parallels between Israel's treatment of Palestinians and "apartheid South Africa," claiming, "In many ways, [Israel] was, and is, worse than South Africa."[65] This questionable comparison omits the fact that South African apartheid was founded on a legally codified system of racial discrimination, whereas Israel's founding documents established a democratic state ensuring full social and political equality for all its citizens. South African apartheid also denied Black South Africans full citizenship, whereas Arab

64. Craig McCarthy, Hannah Flerick, and David Propper, "College Group Zohran Mamdani Co-founded Welcomed Radical Speaker Who Later Blamed US for 9/11 Attacks—'Made Its Bed,'" *New York Post*, July 8, 2025, nypost.com/2025/07/08/us-news/college-group-zohran-mamdani-co-founded-welcomed-radical-speaker-who-blamed-us-for-9-11-attacks-made-its-bed/.

65. Carly Silver, "Reporting Live from the First-Ever SJP National Conference," *New Voices*, October 15, 2011, newvoices.org/2011/10/15/reporting-live-from-the-first-ever-sjp-national-conference/.

Israeli citizens today have full citizenship, including the right to vote and serve in the Knesset, the Israeli parliament. Mahmood further asserted that Israel admired the United States for its historical treatment of Indigenous populations, arguing, "The Zionists think of that particular part of American history as inspirational."[66] This quote not only sheds light on the ideologies shared in the Mamdani household, but it also illustrates the old adage, "Like father, like son," where a son follows the ideology carved by his father.

Zohran Mamdani's background, undoubtedly influenced by his father's ideologies, motivated him to maneuver in the civil sphere in ways that mirror the goals of communism. Prior to his tenure as New York City's mayor, Mamdani worked as a "housing counselor" for "low-income homeowners of color" in Queens. His work involved "negotiating with banks that valued profits over people" and fighting against "decades of pro-corporate policies enacted across [America] as well as [New York]."[67] His biography aligns his professional life with his antipathy for capitalism, which has led to accusations of outright communism, a label he denies despite his ideas and rhetoric. At the 2021 Young Democratic Socialists of America conference, Mamdani urged attendees not to compromise on goals such as "seizing the means of production," a direct echo of language found in Marx's *Communist Manifesto*.[68] In the same breath, he stressed, in Manichaean and Orwellian fashion, the need for attendees to "organize for what is correct and what is right," leaving no nuance

---

66. Ibid.

67. New York Assembly, "Assemblymember—Zohran K. Mamdani—Assembly District 36," New York Assembly, n.d., nyassembly.gov/mem/Zohran-K-Mamdani.

68. Alec Schemmel, "Video Surfaces of Mamdani Using Slogan Rooted in Communist Revolutionary Language," *Fox News*, June 30, 2025, www.foxnews.com/politics/mamdani-under-fire-over-resurfaced-2021-video-endorsing-socialist-goals.

for discussions on what is "correct" or "right" and coercing attendees to accept his version of "correctness" and "rightness."[69]

Assessing whether Mamdani is an anti-American communist gains further traction by evaluating his policy proposals. His controversial positions in the run-up to the 2025 mayoral election included defunding the police, abolishing the prison system, banning all guns, decriminalizing sex work, ending cash bail, decriminalizing drug possession, ending cooperation with ICE, and advocating for the creation of city-owned grocery stores to lower food costs. These policies, particularly the city-owned grocery stores, drew fierce criticism, with Ryan Bourne, a leading economist at the Cato Institute, a libertarian think tank, noting that government-run entities like city-owned grocery stores have "no market discipline" and "no need to earn profits, compete, or serve customers efficiently," which, Bourne stated, leads to "bloated costs, empty shelves, and zero accountability."[70] Local critics of Mamdani's proposals, including high-profile Greek American businessman John Catsimatidis, also raised the "red flag" about this communist-style economic plan, with Catsimatidis warning, "If the city of New York is going socialist, I will definitely close, or sell, or move."[71] During his inauguration speech in January 2026, Mamdani again demonstrated his anti-capitalism, pro-communism worldview when he stated that he would "replace the frigidity of rugged individualism with the warmth of collectivism." Writing for the Cato Institute, Bourne again unpacks Mamdani's ideas, claiming that his use of "collectivism" is "not a slip of the tongue or a vague moral appeal to kindness." Rather, Bourne claims it is a loaded ideological term that

---

69. Ibid.

70. Amanda Macias, "Mamdani's Public Grocery Stores May Have Devastating Effects on City's Food Supply," *Fox New Business*, June 30, 2025, www.foxbusiness.com/politics/mamdanis-public-grocery-stores-may-have-devastating-effects-citys-food-supply.

71. Ibid.

means "a social order in which the claims of the group—often defined and enforced by the state—override individual choice, property rights, and voluntary exchange."[72] As Bourne concludes, "this is not a caricature; it is the standard definition of what is espoused in fascist, socialist, and communist literature."

While these policies may not overtly link to the Islamist goal of supporting Hamas and condemning Israel, they nevertheless position Western capitalism, driven by America and Israel, as "evil" and communism as "good," which is dubious given David Horowitz's accurate reflection on the dangers of communism:

> The catastrophe of Communism included the creation of a totalitarian state; the reintroduction of slave labor on an epic scale; and politically induced famines and government-created poverty of unprecedented proportions; political purges and mass executions resulting in the deaths of an estimated 100 million people. These were the direct results of a system based on socialist theories, which provided no rational method for allocating resources and no effective work incentives, and no guarantees of individual rights. The unique cause of the system's failure was in fact the socialist theories that inspired its creation and that had produced a continent-size theory that did not work.[73]

Honestly examining the outcomes from communist systems since their inception in the nineteenth century raises too many "red flags" to count here. Instead of fostering a society free from discrimination and exploitation, historical evidence shows that communism—with its pervasive system of state control and the negation of individual rights—has led to suffering and widespread economic hardship. It appears, nevertheless, that Mamdani's advocacy for communist-style politics, and the

72. Ryan Bourne, "Mamdani's Collectivism," *Cato at Liberty* (Blog), Cato Institute, January 6, 2026, www.cato.org/blog/mamdani-collectivism.
73. Horowitz, *Unholy Alliance*, 55.

support he garners among progressive "foot soldiers" (students) and even moderately liberal circles, are propelled by a perceived "righteousness" and conviction that society and history move in the "right" direction only through opposition to capitalism and the U.S.-Israel alliance.

It is on the issue of Israel, Zionism, and antisemitism that Mamdani has drawn the sharpest criticism from supporters of the U.S.-Israel alliance. He has repeatedly stated that he does not recognize Israel's right to exist as a Jewish and democratic state,[74] denouncing it as racist and ethnocentric—a standard he does not evenly apply to the dozens of Islamist countries worldwide, many of which systematically treat non-Muslims as second-class citizens under dhimmi status. Mamdani's stance becomes even clearer through his longstanding support for the Boycott, Divestment, and Sanctions (BDS) movement against Israel. On his very first day in office as mayor, he revoked executive orders that had restricted New York City officials from participating in boycotts of Israel. He has also defended the slogan "globalize the intifada" as merely expressing a "desperate desire for equality"—an Orwellian reframing that sanitizes calls for violence against Jews and Israelis.

Another contentious strategy in Mamdani's maneuvering within the "soft war" is his advocacy for "defunding the police," a tactic popularized by BLM, a group whose Flatbush, New York City branch—Equality for Flatbush—endorsed Mamdani's candidacy for mayor in 2025.[75] In a December 2024 X post, Mamdani pledged to "disband" the New York

74. American Jewish Committee, "AJC Expresses Alarm over NYC Mayoral Candidate Zohran Mamdani's Continued Problematic Rhetoric," October 17, 2025, www.ajc.org/news/ajc-expresses-alarm-over-nyc-mayoral-candidate-zohran-mamdanis-continued-problematic-rhetoric.

75. Francesca Walker, "Equality for Flatbush (E4F) Endorses Zohran Mamdani for NYC Mayor," Equality for Flatbush, July 1, 2025, www.equalityforflatbush.org/press-releases-and-statements/equality-for-flatbush-e4f-endorses-zohran-mamdani-for-nyc-mayor/.

City Police Department's Strategic Response Group (SRG), a specialized unit for disorder response and crowd control, which would conveniently give groups like SJP and TPF greater freedom to cause chaos on campuses and American streets.[76] He justified his proposal by arguing that the SRG "brutalized countless New Yorkers exercising their First Amendment rights," a framing that again exemplifies the Orwellian tactic of manipulating language to control the narrative and distort reality. By accusing the "system" of transgressions it is not guilty of, Mamdani mirrors the strategic misdirection that Orwell critiqued, much like how student activists at Columbia University disguised their disorderly tactics—such as seizing Columbia University's Hamilton Hall and "shutting down" the university's library—under the banner of "freedom of speech." Mamdani's deployment of these tactics serves to undermine established institutions and advance the Leftist-Islamist alliance's agenda by twisting the facts and controlling the very definition of truth.

Here, it is worth returning to Mamdani's "ritzy" wedding celebration in his native Uganda, equipped with a high-level security detail and armed guards protecting his family and friends. While he advocates for dismantling elements of the New York City Police Department, he secures important security measures for himself. His contradictory "champagne socialist" lifestyle mirrors Patrisse Cullors, the BLM co-founder who used more than $800,000 in donations to pay her brother for "security services" even though he seems to mostly work as a "graffiti artist."[77]

---

76. Peter Pinedo, "Flashback—Zohran Mamdani Pledged to 'Disband' Key Police Unit That Handles Mass Shootings," *Fox News*, July 29, 2025, www.foxnews.com/politics/flashback-zohran-mamdani-pledged-disband-key-police-unit-handles-mass-shootings.

77. Isabel Vincent and Marjorie Hernandez, "BLM Paid Co-founder Patrisse Cullors' Graffiti Artist Brother $800K for 'Security,'" *New York Post*, May 18, 2022, nypost.com/2022/05/18/blm-paid-patrisse-cullors-graffiti-artist-brother-800k-for-security/.

According to reports, Cullors also purchased a 6,500-square-foot home in California with more than half a dozen bedrooms and bathrooms, a soundstage, a pool, a bungalow, and parking for more than 20 cars.[78] The California property was allegedly purchased for nearly $6 million in cash in October 2020 with money that had been donated to Black Lives Matter. These kinds of contradictions draw criticism from conservative and Republican circles, who claim that Mamdani—and other progressive politicians—are maneuvering in a fashion similar to the pigs in *Animal Farm* that gave way to the infamous line, "Some animals are more equal than others." The U.S. Department of Justice has taken notice as well, launching investigations[79] into BLM leaders for allegedly defrauding donors who contributed more than $90 million during the 2020 "racial justice" protests.

ALEXANDRIA OCASIO-CORTEZ: THE SERGEANT OF AMERICA'S PROGRESSIVE FRONT

Established in 1991, the Congressional Progressive Caucus (CPC), the second-largest Democratic caucus in the House of Representatives, represents the "progressive" faction of the Democratic Party, comprising nearly one hundred members from the House of Representatives and one senator (Bernie Sanders). Its "official" agenda highlights mainstream political issues like immigration reform, healthcare, the economy, and

78. Jesse Silverstein, "Black Lives Matter's $6 Million Dollar House," Intelligencer (blog), *New York Magazine*, April 12, 2022, nymag.com/intelligencer/2022/04/black-lives-matter-6-million-dollar-house.html.

79. Associated Press, "Justice Department Investigating Fraud Allegations Against Black Lives Matter Leaders, AP Sources Say," *PBS NewsHour*, October 30, 2025, www.pbs.org/newshour/nation/justice-department-investigating-fraud-allegations-against-black-lives-matter-leaders-ap-sources-say.

climate. Beneath this public-facing mandate, however, the CPC operates as a leading entity within the Leftist-Islamist alliance. While the roles of former CPC deputy co-chair Omar and former CPC vice chair Tlaib have already been examined as high-ranking pieces on our metaphorical chessboard, Alexandria Ocasio-Cortez (AOC), a New York City socialist representative and executive board member of the caucus, stands out as a pivotal, albeit lower-ranked strategic player in the alliance.

AOC's position is akin to a "sergeant" in military terms, serving just below the ranks of the commander and lieutenant. Her specific role is, in part, shaped by the rigid construction of "representation" rooted in identity politics, a progressive framework that, as I have often encountered in my own advocacy and publications, wants only certain kinds of people to represent certain groups of people. While she is a Hispanic woman, a "marginalized" identity in Leftist circles, she does not possess the "right" identity markers to serve in the upper echelons of the Leftist-Islamist alliance. AOC is neither Palestinian nor Muslim, meaning she cannot effectively lead the troops in battle. This dynamic, which dismisses objectivity and neutrality in favor of subjectivity and ideology, is a dangerous tactic guiding the Leftist-Islamist alliance, because it creates ideological boundaries that preclude more nuanced discourse, which is crucial for a healthy civic nation.

Turning to AOC's public pronouncements, including the typical Leftist-Islamist rhetoric of accusing Israel of "genocide" against the Palestinians, we see that AOC has accused Israel of "forced famine" in Gaza, claiming it was "beyond our ability to deny or explain [it] away."[80] Here, we discern a clear touch of Orwellianism, as AOC attempts to coercively enforce a singular "truth" by implying that those who disagree with her statement are living in an alternate reality. Her statement on the

80. Michelle Shen and Aileen Graef, "Ocasio-Cortez Defends Accusing Israel of Genocide in Floor Speech," *CNN*, March 24, 2024, www.cnn.com/2024/03/24/politics/alexandria-ocasio-cortez-aoc-israel-gaza-genocide-cnntv.

Gaza crisis also placed blame entirely on Israel, claiming that "14,000 babies face severe malnutrition if the Israeli government does not reverse course."[81] Her statement further added, "We must pressure the Israeli government to open up more routes for humanitarian aid and finally uphold the law by stopping further weapons transfers to Israel." While alleviating famine is paramount for humanity, AOC focused solely on Israel and not Hamas. Her convictions are problematic as they place no pressure on, and make no reference to, Hamas's own tactics of shaping public opinion to portray Israel as the sole "oppressor," despite evidence that Hamas itself oppresses Palestinians, profits from humanitarian aid, including food, by reselling it on the "black market," and otherwise maintains control over the civilian population.

AOC's strategic maneuvers on the political terrain, like those of her progressive colleagues, extend beyond international policy to direct engagement with "foot soldiers." She joined Mahmoud Khalil, the Columbia graduate detained by Immigration and Customs Enforcement (ICE) in 2025, as a key speaker at a press conference immediately following his release. She claimed his detention was a violation of his First Amendment rights, referring to Khalil as a "prisoner" whose detention, she asserted, "had no grounds" and was politically motivated because he advocates for "Palestinianism."[82] She added that he has been "accused baselessly of horrific allegations" simply because "our overall establishment disagrees with his political speech."

AOC's support for Khalil's release provoked significant anger in Re-

---

81. Alexandria Ocasio-Cortez, press Release, May 21, 2025, ocasio-cortez.house.gov/media/press-releases/ocasio-cortez-statement-worsening-humanitarian-crisis-gaza.

82. Naomi La Chance, "Mahmoud Khalil Says He'll 'Continue to Protest' Following ICE Detention Release," *Rolling Stone*, June 21, 2025, www.rollingstone.com/politics/politics-news/mahmoud-khalil-aoc-ice-release-trump-1235369571/.

publican circles, which accused her of side-stepping critically important facts regarding Khalil's detention.[83] There are two primary issues with AOC's position—first, Khalil's deportation was justified under section 237(a)(1)(A) of the Immigration and Nationality Act for willfully misrepresenting facts on his Form I-485 application for adjusting his green card status.[84] Immigration Judge James E. Comans determined that Khalil failed to disclose his involvement with the United Nations Relief and Works Agency for Palestine Refugees (UNRWA), whose members participated in the October 7 attacks,[85] a British Embassy–funded research office focused on Syria, and Columbia University Apartheid Divest (CUAD), the student group that played a central organizing role in pro-Palestinian protests.[86] Judge Comans deemed these omissions intentional and ordered his removal. Second, AOC's remarks exemplify both Marxism and Orwellianism. Regarding the former, her mention of "our overall establishment" points to Marx's call to dismantle existing systems ruled by the "elite." In relation to Orwell, her remarks speak to the manipulation of language and an attempt to control the narrative about Khalil's activities by presenting them merely as a "free speech" issue. AOC also employs a Gramscian "war of position" tactic in these statements by shifting the "hegemonic" understanding of Khalil's actions from "illegal" to "legal." By positioning his activities as "pro-American"—implying that if one is pro–freedom of speech, one should be

83. Ibid.

84. James E. Comans, "In the Matter of Mahmoud Khalil, in Removal Proceedings," Immigration Court, Oakdale, Louisiana, September 12, 2025, storage.courtlistener.com/recap/gov.uscourts.njd.564334/gov.uscourts.njd.564334.378.0.pdf.

85. Ronny Reyes, "UN Admits Nine UNRWA Staffers 'May Have Been Involved' in Oct. 7 Attack on Israel," *New York Post*, August 5, 2024, nypost.com/2024/08/05/world-news/un-admits-nine-unrwa-staffers-may-have-been-involved-in-oct-7-attack-on-israel/.

86. Comans, "In the Matter of Mahmoud Khalil, in Removal Proceedings."

pro-Khalil—AOC sidesteps his disruptive activities, effectively elevating him to a "war hero" in the Leftist-Islamist alliance, and a near "martyr" for its causes.

UNITED AGAINST THE U.S.–ISRAEL ALLIANCE: A SPECTRUM OF LEFTIST GROUPS AND ISLAMIST ALLIES

In addition to individual politicians, a number of organizations under the umbrella of the Democratic Party also play a significant role in the Leftist-Islamist alliance. While these subparties may not command immediate recognition in the broader American consciousness, they nonetheless constitute important components within the wider "progressive" movement. These entities wield significant ideological force and provide material support to Democrats, primarily through their strategic endorsements, active campaigning, and dedicated grassroots organizing. Some of these subparties possess deep historical roots in American political discourse, while others have only recently become associated with radicalization and even violence. What unites them is a shared ideological alignment with Marxism, an alignment that serves to further the cause of Islamism.

The first subparty within the progressive movement to be addressed is the Party for Socialism and Liberation (PSL), a Marxist political entity that believes "For the planet to live capitalism must end." It advocates for overturning the "capitalist state," resisting "imperialist domination," and abridging the First Amendment "in the efforts to eliminate racism, xenophobia, and all forms of bigotry."[87] On August 16, 2024, the PSL joined other Leftist and Islamist organizations by signing a letter to John Whitmire, the mayor of Houston, Texas, regarding his comment

87. Party for Socialism and Liberation, "About the Party for Socialism and Liberation," n.d., pslweb.org/about/

that protesters were supported by "Iranian cells" in America.[88] The letter claimed that Mayor Whitmire's comments were "Islamophobic rhetoric," a defense that attempted to silence any criticism of the Leftist-Islamist alliance's network as "racism" or "bigotry." The signees of the letter were a "who's who" of the Leftist-Islamist alliance in Houston: CAIR-Houston, Rice-SJP, the University of Houston-SJP, Houston for Palestinian Liberation, and the Palestinian Youth Movement, among others.

The PSL is an immediate example of the consequences arising from the convergence of Leftist and Islamist ideologies. Elias Rodriguez, who killed Yaron Lischinsky and Sarah Milgrim, was linked to the PSL. In a 2017 article in *Liberation Magazine*, a PSL publication, Rodriguez was quoted as railing against a proposed Amazon headquarters in Chicago, claiming that "[Amazon's] whitening of Seattle is structurally racist and a direct danger to all workers who live in that city."[89] Like Rodriguez, the PSL espouses a worldview that fuses CRT, anti-capitalism, and anti-Zionism. Its positions stand as a grim illustration of the current crisis facing American society: ideological extremism is translating into deadly violence, a new intifada. The group's support for the global intifada and its anti-capitalist views might appear to be separate strategies, as one critiques economic systems, while the other takes a militant stance against the actions of the state of Israel. However, as the *Jerusalem Post* reported, these two positions "often feed off each other, sharing a common narrative that blames a small, powerful group [Jews] for global suffering and

---

88. Houston for Palestinian Liberation, "'Protestors Are Being Paid by Iran'—A Statement in Response to Whitmire's Islamophobic Rhetoric," Houston for Palestinian Liberation, Instagram, post dated August 16, 2024, www.instagram.com/p/C-vTGUCp1kn/?hl=en&img_index=4.

89. Grace Wilson, "Washington Shooting Suspect Was Anti-Israel Activist, Railed Against Seattle's 'Whitening,'" *Times of Israel*, May 23, 2025, www.timesofisrael.com/washington-shooting-suspect-was-anti-israel-activist-railed-against-seattles-whitening/.

injustice."[90] This shared narrative, which is central to the Leftist-Islamist alliance, draws heavily on antisemitic conspiracy theories that repackage old stereotypes as criticism of "Zionists," "globalists," and "bankers." Given this narrative, the PSL is a natural ally of Islamist organizations.

While there is no direct organizational equivalent to the PSL in Europe, several Marxist-Leninist groups actively participate in pro-Palestinian protests and actively disseminate anti-capitalist and "anti-imperialist" messaging. The Workers' Party of Belgium (PTB/PVDA) is the most prominent among them, with its hard-left Marxist ideology and its push for sanctioning Israel, justified in the name of "resistance." From the outbreak of the Israel-Hamas war in October 2023 onward, the PTB played a key role in organizing large-scale pro-Palestinian demonstrations in Brussels. These protests frequently drew crowds in the tens of thousands, with organizers sometimes claiming as many as 110,000 participants. The demonstrations typically portrayed Israel's military campaign in Gaza as "genocide" and framed Palestinian armed groups —including Hamas—as legitimate "resistance" against occupation and imperialism.

Party leaders such as General Secretary Peter Mertens and MEP Marc Botenga repeatedly accused Belgium, the European Union, and the West at large of complicity in Israeli actions through economic, military, and political support, describing their activities as a continuation of Western imperialism in the Middle East. This kind of "pro-resistance" rhetoric helped the PTB mobilize support within Belgium's Muslim communities,[91] particularly among Arab and Turkish populations in Brussels and Antwerp, where anti-Israel fervor is leading to a rise of

---

90. Michael J. Salamon and Louis Libin, "Anti-Capitalism, Antisemitism, and the Global Intifada—A Troubling Link in Washington," *Jerusalem Post*, June 1, 2025, www.jpost.com/opinion/article-856156.

91. Thomas O'Reilly, "Communists Top the Polls in Brussels, Backed by Muslim Vote," *European Conservative*, February 22, 2024.

Islamism. As rooks on the European political chessboard, PTB leaders used sustained street mobilization to influence the broader public and put political pressure on the Belgian government. In early September 2025, the government announced that Belgium would recognize the State of Palestine at the United Nations General Assembly and imposed a package of twelve sanctions on Israel.[92]

PSL "foot soldiers" and their PTB comrades across the Atlantic Ocean also have support from the Communist Party USA (CPUSA), which was founded in 1919 in the aftermath of the Bolshevik Revolution. The CPUSA's style of "communism" is not the style of communism that Americans were familiar with during the Cold War. While still upholding Marxist principles, the party has abandoned its former strategy of overthrowing the U.S. government, instead focusing on collaborating with other progressive movements in an effort to spread "cultural Marxism" in the civil sphere. Yet, despite its repositioning, the CPUSA still targets the same enemies. Horowitz noted, "All that really distinguishes this Neo-Communist perspective from its Communism predecessor is its ad hoc attitude towards the revolutionary future, and the nihilistic agendas that follow."[93] He added, "The contemporary Left defines itself and organizes its unity as a movement *against* rather than *for*," with capitalism and Zionism as its primary targets. The CPUSA repeatedly condoned the campus protests and the occupation of university grounds.[94] The party's statements provided solidarity to the students by defending their "democratic right to organize and protest," echoing familiar Leftist

---

92. Al Jazeera, "Belgium to Recognise Palestinian Statehood, Impose Sanctions on Israel," *Al Jazeera*, September 2, 2025, www.aljazeera.com/news/2025/9/2/belgium-to-recognise-palestine-at-un-general-assembly-foreign-minister.
93. Horowitz, *Unholy Alliance*, 59.
94. Communist Party USA, "CP Clubs Support Student Protests Against Gaza Genocide," May 16, 2024, cpusa.org/article/cp-clubs-support-student-protests-against-gaza-genocide/.

rhetoric, all while decrying the "Israeli-led genocidal war against Gaza."[95]

The CPUSA is a marginal political player and the group has little, if any, electoral impact. The European context, however, shows a significantly different landscape, with communist parties remaining relevant in several EU countries. For example, Europe's strongest communist party, the Communist Party of Greece (KKE), received about 7% of the Greek vote in the 2024 elections.

The alignment between CPUSA and the "foot soldiers" at U.S. universities underscores the diverse range of groups willing to collaborate under the banner of Jew hatred, furthering the argument that the Leftist-Islamist alliance is driven by ideological connections and shared political objectives. The fact that progressive subparties like the PSL and CPUSA operate so publicly in the civil sphere reveals a Gramscian tactic of operating "within the system" to achieve one's aims and goals. Two demonstrations at Arizona State University (ASU) are a case in point. Representatives of CPUSA and the PSL gave speeches at an SJP demonstration at ASU in 2024, which included a list of Boycott, Divestment, Sanctions (BDS) movement demands presented to ASU's leaders.[96] A year earlier, ASU students across disparate activist groups on campus united in support of Hamas's attacks on Israel, with SJP and the Movimiento Estudiantil Chicano de Aztlán (MEChA), a movement shaped by Marxist principles of "liberation" and "anti-capitalism," leading the protest.[97] Others involved in the protest included the CPUSA-Phoenix

---

95. Communist Party USA, "Campus Ceasefire Protests Deserve Support—Keep the Pressure On!" April 23, 2024, www.cpusa.org/article/campus-ceasefire-protests-deserve-support-keep-the-pressure-on/.

96. Sophia Ramirez, "ASU Administrator Collects SJP Petition At Protest On Tempe Campus," *State Press*, January 19, 2024, www.statepress.com/article/2024/01/palestine-protest-barrett.

97. Arizona Daily Independent, "ASU MEChA Behind Pro-Hamas Activism

and PSL-Phoenix. Around the time of this protest, the MEChA called for a "revolution" in an Instagram post that read, "Death to the 'Israeli' entity! Death to the 'American' entity! Long live Palestine! Long live Turtle Island!" "Turtle Island" references the Native American myth that North and Central America were formed on the back of a turtle.[98]

These ASU cases illustrate the complete convergence of the Leftist-Islamist alliance. The "foot soldiers" or "pawns"—students and activists—actively demonstrate on campus, their motivations shaped through the "ideological training" that they receive from "bishops"—professors whose academic theories are rooted in Marxism. Concurrently, the "knights"—various organizations within the civil sphere—engage in orchestrating and bolstering these university demonstrations. This not only emboldens the "foot soldiers" but also normalizes Marxist discourse within the public consciousness, which Islamists strategically promote to advance their own agenda of delegitimizing Israel and transforming not just America but also the broader West.

THE REPUBLICAN PUSHBACK: DESIGNATING THE MUSLIM BROTHERHOOD A TERRORIST ORGANIZATION

The progressive movement's embrace of Leftist-Islamist ideas and activism is perceived by many Americans as a grave concern and potential threat to social cohesion and the general well-being of the United States. While this chapter has outlined this intensifying phenomenon, it is equally important to examine efforts to push back against these intertwined ideologies, including a growing movement within Congress, pri-

---

Calls For Revolution, Death to America," *Arizona Daily Independent*, October 19, 2023, arizonadailyindependent.com/2023/10/19/asu-mecha-behind-pro-hamas-activism-calls-for-revolution-death-to-america/.

98. Ibid.

marily among members of the Republican Party, to formally designate the Muslim Brotherhood, the overseeing faction of the Leftist-Islamist alliance, as a terrorist organization.

Founded in 1928 by Hassan al-Banna, an Egyptian Islamist, the Muslim Brotherhood emerged as an opponent of "Western influence" and an advocate for "Islamic governing principles" at all levels of society. Throughout its history, the Muslim Brotherhood has experienced a fluctuating trajectory, rising to the pinnacle of Egyptian politics with its electoral victory during the Arab Spring in 2011. It is currently an invasive transnational network across much of the West, including in the United States, with direct and indirect links to SJP, AMP, CAIR, and Islamic Relief USA.

The urgency of designating the Muslim Brotherhood as a "terrorist organization" is highlighted by a 2023 Institute for the Study of Global Antisemitism and Policy (ISGAP) report, which noted that Hamas, upon its creation, explicitly designated itself as "one of the wings of [Muslim] Brotherhood in Palestine."[99] This push for designation echoed efforts from President Donald Trump's first term, during which groundwork was laid to sanction the Brotherhood's global affiliates, though a formal designation never materialized.[100] However, congressional momentum to formally designate the group as a terrorist organization began in earnest in June 2025 when the ISGAP participated in a congressional briefing focused on developing strategies to address its threat.

---

99. Institute for the Study of Global Antisemitism and Policy, "The Qatari Regime, Hamas and the Muslim Brotherhood—The Globalisation of Antisemitism and Antidemocracy," 2023, isgap.org/wp-content/uploads/2023/11/QATAR-REGIME_HAMAS_MB_FINAL.pdf.

100. Adam Kredo, "Trump Admin, Congress Ready to Designate Muslim Brotherhood a Terror Group," *Washington Free Beacon*, May 1, 2019, freebeacon.com/national-security/trump-admin-congress-ready-to-designate-muslim-brotherhood-a-terror-group/.

Following the hearing, Senator Ted Cruz, a Texas Republican and consistent proponent of bold strategic action against the Muslim Brotherhood, asserted that the Muslim Brotherhood "uses political violence to achieve political ends and destabilize American allies, both within countries and across national boundaries."[101] He further claimed that the Brotherhood "used the Biden administration to consolidate and deepen their influence," emphasizing that the "Trump administration and a Republican Congress cannot afford to avoid the threat that they pose to Americans and American national security." Following the hearing, Representative Nancy Mace, a Republican from South Carolina, introduced the "Muslim Brotherhood Is a Terrorist Organization Act," a proposed bill that calls for formally designating the Muslim Brotherhood as a Foreign Terrorist Organization (FTO) under Section 219 of the Immigration and Nationality Act. Mace noted in her official statement, "The Muslim Brotherhood does not just support terrorism, it inspires it."[102] As these statements suggest, the threat to U.S. national security comes not only from the Muslim Brotherhood but also from its allies in "progressive" circles that engage in similar anti-American and antisemitic rhetoric and that similarly seek to subvert foundational American values and principles.

There are several methods through which the Muslim Brotherhood might be formally classified as a foreign terrorist organization. In addition to the FTO route, a second option entails adding the Muslim Brotherhood to the Specially Designated Global Terrorist (SDGT)

---

101. Adam Kredo, "Congress Nears Move to Designate the Muslim Brotherhood as a Terrorist Organization," *Washington Free Beacon*, June 3, 2025, freebeacon.com/national-security/congress-nears-move-to-designate-the-muslim-brotherhood-as-a-terrorist-organization/.

102. Nancy Mace, "Rep. Nancy Mace Targets Muslim Brotherhood with New Bill," U.S. House of Representatives, June 10, 2025, mace.house.gov/media/press-releases/rep-nancy-mace-targets-muslim-brotherhood-new-bill.

organization list, which carries similar financial penalties. Such designations would not only serve as a strong declarative stance against the Muslim Brotherhood but also provide tangible tools to disrupt its financial networks and curb its influence in the academic and civil spheres. To counter the Brotherhood, Congress should also keep scrutinizing SJP, given its direct ties to American Muslims for Palestine (AMP), an organization accused of financing groups like Hamas (see chapter 3). Previous oversight of SJP has included a May 2024 request by sixteen Republican senators that the Internal Revenue Service (IRS) investigate nonprofit organizations providing financial support to SJP.[103] The letter specifically named Westchester People's Action Coalition (Wespac) and the Tides Foundation, two progressive donors, and the Americans for Justice in Palestine Educational Foundation (AJP), a branch of AMP, as warranting investigation. The Republican senators alleged potential violations of these groups' tax-exempt status due to SJP's vocal support for Hamas, arguing that SJP's demonstrations and rhetoric potentially constituted material support for terrorism, which disqualifies nonprofit organizations from tax-exempt status.

European countries, as noted earlier, have taken steps to ban or heavily restrict Muslim Brotherhood–linked groups from operating on the European continent. The big question is whether France will decide to follow in their footsteps. A May 2025 report commissioned by the French government warned that the MB poses a long-term threat to national cohesion through a strategy of subtle "entryism" to create "Islamist ecosystems."[104] The report authors added that the Brotherhood,

---

103. Luke Tress, "Republican Senators Demand IRS Investigate Sponsor of Students for Justice in Palestine," *Times of Israel*, May 14, 2024, www.timesofisrael.com/republican-senators-demand-irs-investigate-sponsor-of-students-for-justice-in-palestine/.

104. Ministère de l'Intérieur, Frères musulmans et islamisme politique en France (report, Paris: République Française, 2025), www.interieur.gouv.fr/sites/

led by the Federation of Muslims of France, seeks to infiltrate schools, mosques, institutions, civil society organizations, and local governments from the bottom up, all with financial and ideological support from Turkey and Qatar.

The convergence of campus activism ("foot soldiers"), revolutionary rhetoric ("ideological training"), and the operational capacity of Muslim Brotherhood–affiliated entities operating in the civil sphere reveals that SJP is much more than a "student movement." Progressive politicians like Tlaib, Omar, Mamdani, and AOC may maneuver around the "battlefield" in a way that furthers the cause of the Leftist-Islamist alliance, but Republican members of Congress are equally able to maneuver by introducing legislation and launching investigations as part of their strategy in the "soft war."

THE CHESSBOARD OF AMERICAN POLITICS: FROM PROGRESSIVE ROOKS TO THE ULTIMATE ARBITERS

As the final pieces settle on the metaphorical chessboard, it is evident that the progressive politicians, acting as "rooks," have not merely moved across files and ranks, but have also reshaped the terrain of the "soft war." They dictate the ideological battle from the highest echelons of power, transforming abstract Marxist theories into actual policy and divisive rhetoric that furthers the Leftist-Islamist cause. The "progressive" movement, while promising forward momentum, often conceals a strategic regression in which American liberties and securities are eroded by the various entities within the alliance. By focusing on group identities and perceived historical grievances, this strain of progressivism fosters societal division, exacerbates the "us" versus "them" dynamics that align with

---

minint/files/medias/documents/2025-05/2025-05-02-rapport-freres-musulmans.pdf.

Marxist demands and reinforce Manichaean worldviews, and, more importantly, aims to delegitimize foundational American institutions and values.

This trajectory, ironically, bears a resemblance to Marx's own conviction that history progresses through distinct phases, culminating in the "highest" and final stage of communism. The concept of being on the "right side of history," often attributed to Marx, implies a moral and historical imperative to align with forces pushing society forward towards its communist destiny.

Indeed, the pervasive Marxist influence in the progressive movement is noticeable in its very manipulation of historical narratives. Progressive politicians deploy distorted accounts to control public perception of complex issues like the Israel-Palestine conflict. Here, it is imperative to recall Orwell's prescient quote from *Nineteen Eighty-Four*: "Who controls the past controls the future; who controls the present controls the past." This Orwellian principle of controlling the past is most evident in politicians' narratives surrounding Israel. For example, by representing the *nakba* solely as a moment of Palestinian "victimhood" and "mass expulsion," while omitting the historical context of Arab aggression in 1948, progressives like Rashida Tlaib delegitimize Israel's existence, which in turn jeopardizes American interests in the Middle East. Her coordinated actions with other elements of the Leftist-Islamist alliance are integral to the strategic blueprint of the alliance. More than anything, this coordination demonstrates that redefining American identity and delegitimizing Israel can be achieved without ever dropping a bomb or firing a bullet.

As we progress through the "soft war," we now shift our focus to the ultimate arbiters—the international actors—the "kings" and "queens." While progressive politicians possess the powerful capacity to control resources, enact legislation, and shape narratives within public discourse, international players in the Leftist-Islamist alliance wield even greater power. This makes them critically important pieces on the chessboard. Our final transition, therefore, is to the realm of international relations. We will examine the ability of global forces to dictate maneuvers in the "soft war."

CHAPTER 5

SUBVERSIVE GLOBAL FORCES: INTERNATIONAL PLAYERS ON "SOFT WAR" BATTLEFIELDS

Finally, we turn to the international players—the "kings" and "queens" of the metaphorical chessboard. These state and nonstate actors wield the most power and are the ultimate arbiters of the "soft war." The geopolitical realities of this specific battlefield are captured by the adage "The enemy of my enemy is my friend," whereby two groups that might otherwise be neutral toward one another, if not outright enemies, have forged a strategic partnership based on a shared opposition to a common foe and a desire to weaken or defeat mutual adversaries. For Leftists, the "enemy" is "capitalist exploitation," "neo-colonialism," "systematic oppression," and "white supremacy." For Islamists, the "enemy" is any force that has been a source of "historical oppression" and that poses a direct challenge to "Islamic supremacy." This global dimension of the "soft war" transforms the Leftist-Islamist alliance from a localized or national phenomenon to an expansive, interconnected, and dangerous transnational network capable of providing informational, logistical, ideological, strategic, and financial support to aligned groups. What should become clear by the end of the chapter is that the alliance is backed by powerful international players—from Hamas and Qatar to Iran and China. These authoritarian regimes and countries represent some of the world's most repressive systems, exposing the hypocrisy of Leftists who champion "human rights" and "anti-racism" while forging tactical alliances with the very forces that systematically crush both.

HAMAS AND THE "NOBLE CAUSE": THE RHETORIC OF RESISTANCE AND REVOLUTION

To understand the international dimensions of this alliance, it is essential to first examine Hamas, the group that provides the core ideological sustenance for the coalition. Without it, the Leftist-Islamist alliance lacks a unifying purpose to galvanize its troops. For many, a "victory" for Hamas is the ultimate triumph against the U.S.-Israel alliance. While a tangible victory might have once been measured by events at "ground zero" in Gaza, it has become increasingly clear that the true battle for hearts and minds can now be won in the ideological arena.

While Israel overwhelmed Gaza with its superior military capabilities following October 7, Hamas arguably emerged victorious on the "public relations" front by convincing many Westerners, especially those of Generation Z, that its violent tactics represent legitimate "resistance" to "colonization" and "occupation" rather than outright terrorism. These kinds of narratives predate the October 7 attack.[1] For example, in a December 2012 speech, Khaled Mashaal, the then-exiled Hamas leader,

1. Gabrielle Fahmy, "More Than 60% of American Gen Z Support Hamas over Israel, Alarming Survey Shows," *New York Post*, August 30, 2025, nypost.com/2025/08/30/world-news/60-of-gen-z-in-us-support-hamas-over-israel-poll/.

reiterated the group's Marxist and Fanonian stance, declaring, "The Palestinian state will be achieved through resistance, not negotiation. Liberation must come first, followed by statehood."[2] Palestine, he asserted, "belongs to us entirely, from the river to the sea, from the south to the north," claiming that the group had the right to use "any means necessary" to fight their so-called oppressors. As noted elsewhere in this book, the slogan "From the River to the Sea, Palestine Will Be Free" implies a desire to annihilate the State of Israel, making it a "genocidal" call to action. His strategy of "by any means necessary" is blatant revolutionary rhetoric, a "call to arms," if you will, the likes of which led Elias Rodriguez to kill Yaron Lischinsky and Sarah Milgrim.

Notice, too, how Mashaal's strategy does not draw upon dialogue, conflict resolution, or peaceful negotiations, but rather on "resistance" in the form of violence. His strategy is condoned by groups such as SJP, CAIR, and TPF, whose actions and messaging reveal that they are ideologically and tactically aligned with a terrorist organization. This alignment demonstrates how the first four components of the alliance, as noted in previous chapters, act as ideological mouthpieces for authoritarian regimes like Hamas, which appropriates the language of "liberation" and "anti-imperialism" to disguise their true motives—the eradication of Israel, the end of U.S. influence in the strategically important Middle East, and the Islamization of Europe.

To further unpack Hamas's role in the Leftist-Islamist alliance, it is necessary to delve into the foundational charters that shape the group's agenda and worldview. Its original 1987 charter asserted a commitment to Marxism by backing the "oppressed," while explicitly stating that violent jihad is the group's "chosen path" and that "death for the sake of Allah is the loftiest of its wishes."[3] With these passages, Hamas replaced

2. Wilson Center, "Doctrine of Hamas," October 20, 2023, www.wilsoncenter.org/article/doctrine-hamas.

3. Ibid.

Marx's "class-based" struggle with a nationalist (Palestinian) and religious (Islamist) one, framing its cause as liberation from Israel's "occupation," a logic it would later use to suppress its own people by denying human rights to Palestinians and rule Gaza with an iron fist.

Beyond these references to Leftist and Islamist ideologies, the 1987 charter also contained overt antisemitic ideas. The charter claimed that Jews used their wealth to seize control of global media outlets, including news agencies, the press, publishing houses, and broadcasting stations, adding that they financed revolutions worldwide to advance Jewish and Israeli interests. The charter repeats age-old antisemitic tropes outlined in the forged 1903 text *The Protocols of the Elders of Zion*, which has been used to incite discrimination and hatred of Jewish people[4] and is often metaphorically described as the "holy grail" of antisemitism because it serves as the ultimate form of conspiracy-based Jew hatred. Hamas's reliance on the text's narratives to justify its agenda stands at the heart of the Leftist-Islamist mission, which is why success in the "soft war" depends on framing and reframing "narratives" and winning support in the public sphere.

Hamas, in Orwellian fashion, later attempted to "soften" and "rebrand" its image through a revised May 2017 charter.[5] A key difference between the two charters is that the latter specifies that Hamas's conflict is with the "Zionist project," not with Jews because of their religion. Namely, the 2017 charter states, "Hamas does not wage a struggle against the Jews because they are Jewish but wages a struggle against the Zionists who occupy Palestine." The reframing of Hamas's mission as "anti-Zionist" rather than "anti-Jewish" is a deceptive tactic designed to reframe a religious and ethnic hatred of Jews into an "anti-imperialist"

---

4. United States Holocaust Memorial Museum, "An Antisemitic Conspiracy—The Protocols of the Elders of Zion," n.d., encyclopedia.ushmm.org/content/en/article/protocols-of-the-elders-of-zion.
5. Wilson Center, "Doctrine of Hamas."

political critique and to win over "good Jews," as Hamas has done with groups like Jewish Voice for Peace (JVP). This strategy of winning over those Hamas views as "acceptable" Jews delegitimizes Zionism, weakens public support for Israel, and creates rifts within the Jewish diaspora. These tactics remind us of the old military strategy of "divide and conquer," which involves breaking an entity into smaller parts and then finding ways to pit them against each other.

Though militarily outmatched in the "hard war," Hamas has found success in the "soft war" by winning over public opinion and reshaping narratives through propaganda. This reality brings to mind a popular term often used to describe those who, perhaps unintentionally, serve a political agenda by uncritically accepting a carefully crafted message. The term "useful idiots" refers to individuals who blindly follow Hamas's narratives without a deeper understanding of the inner workings of Gaza or the dynamics at play with the Leftist-Islamist alliance. Behind the "useful idiots" are often calculating strategists who wield significant power in the "soft war," which is rarely a puppet show for the naïve but rather a carefully orchestrated plan to shape the world to their advantage.

While Hamas provides the ideological and emotional core of the alliance, its efforts could not be sustained without powerful state backers, the most significant of which is Qatar.

DARK CHARITY: QATAR'S FOOTPRINT ON THE LEFTIST-ISLAMIST ALLIANCE

Hamas's entire strategic operation, from Gaza's war zones to the halls of Congress, is underwritten by the state-level funding of Qatar, the small yet disproportionately influential nation that has become a central, if often understated, architect in the international front of the Leftist-Islamist alliance. Despite being the size of Connecticut, Qatar has rapidly emerged as a major global player in the financial and diplomatic worlds, positioning itself as a country with "soft power" on the international stage. Even though Qatar has won praise for its contributions to humanitarian aid and investment, at the same time, it has supported Islamism, condoned Hamas's terrorism, and provided financial support to spread "cultural Marxism" in Western countries. We see the workings of Sun Tzu and Gramsci in the country's strategic maneuvers. Sun Tzu called for winning a war without direct military confrontation, while Gramsci's "war of position" called for infiltrating and reshaping civil society from within to achieve hegemonic control.

The phrase "follow the money" is relevant when examining Qatar's position on the figurative battlefield. Notably, Qatar has provided hundreds of millions of dollars to Gaza over the years,[6] with Israeli reports putting the exact number at $1.1 billion between 2012 and 2018 alone.[7] While Qatar claims this aid is exclusively for "humanitarian" purposes, numerous reports indicate that Hamas frequently diverts Qatar's assistance, redistributes it to Islamist militants, and even sells it back to Palestinians in Gaza.[8] More specifically, intelligence assessments suggest that Qatar's "humanitarian aid" to Gaza was used, in part, to fund Hamas's extensive tunnel network. This subterranean infrastructure gave the group the ability to engage in asymmetric warfare against the Israeli

6. Nima Elbagir, Barbara Arvanitidis, Alex Platt, Raja Razek, Nadeem Ebrahim, CNN, and Uri Blau, "Qatar Sent Millions to Gaza for Years—with Israel's Backing. Here's What We Know about the Controversial Deal," *CNN*, December 12, 2023, www.cnn.com/2023/12/11/middleeast/qatar-hamas-funds-israel-backing-intl.

7. Stuart Winer, "Qatar Gave over $1.1 billion to Gaza Strip from 2012–18, Ministers Told," *Times of Israel*, February 11, 2019, www.timesofisrael.com/qatar-gave-over-1-1-billion-to-gaza-strip-over-six-years-report/.

8. Lazar Berman, "IDF Says Documents Show Hamas Has Been Confiscating Aid as a Matter of Policy," *Times of Israel*, June 13, 2025, www.timesofisrael.com/idf-says-documents-show-hamas-has-been-confiscating-aid-as-a-matter-of-policy/.

military after October 7.[9] Beyond this "money trail," Qatar has offered refuge to Hamas's political leadership, including Ismail Haniyeh, its former leader. Before his assassination by Israel, Qatar provided him a secure operational base from which he could travel internationally, engage in diplomatic activities, and manage Hamas's financial networks.[10] All of these maneuvers significantly benefit Hamas, not only by expanding the group's financial resources but also by freeing up its military assets, thereby directly supporting the Leftist-Islamist objective of eliminating Israel.

Qatar's financial and diplomatic backing for Hamas hints at the country's broader "soft power" strategy, which extends to considerable investments in U.S. institutions, primarily its top universities. Currently, Qatar contributes more funds to universities in the United States than any other country,[11] primarily through the Qatar Foundation, a government-run entity. The foundation changed its identity in 2006 to present itself as a private organization without any restrictions tied to a government entity, while the Al Thani royal family retained ownership. As a result, Qatar was able to mask state funding as private-sector giving.[12] The country's donations ramped up significantly during President Joe Biden's administration, with a third of Qatar's donations—over $2 billion—giv-

9. Ruth Marks Eglash, "How Hamas Fooled Gullible Donors to Fund Its Billion-Dollar Terror Tunnel System," *Fox News*, January 14, 2024, www.foxnews.com/world/hamas-fooled-gullible-donors-fund-billion-dollar-terror-tunnel-system.

10. Seth J. Frantzman, "Qatar's Bait and Switch Game as Mediator and Host—Analysis," *Jerusalem Post*, August 2, 2024, www.jpost.com/middle-east/article-828300.

11. Charles Asher Small, "Fueling Chaos—Tracing the Flow of Tax-Exempt Dollars to Antisemitism," United States House Committee on Ways and Means, July 23, 2024, waysandmeans.house.gov/wp-content/uploads/2024/07/Small-Testimony.pdf.

12. Ibid.

en between 2021 and 2024.[13] The U.S. Department of Education reported[14] that in 2025 alone, Qataris invested $1.1 billion in American universities, making Qatar the largest donor in the world. In the European context, Qatar has similarly provided large sums of funds to European universities, though the scale is smaller than the country's investments in U.S. higher education. While other Gulf states such as the United Arab Emirates have also provided millions in funding to Western universities, there is a crucial distinction—the U.A.E. is a signatory to the Abraham Accords and has normalized relations with Israel, placing it on the opposite side of the "soft war" from Qatar. One country works toward peaceful cooperation with Israelis, while the other seeks to malign and, in the worst cases, destroy them.

These developments have drawn the attention of investigative media like *The Free Press* and "watchdog" organizations like Zachor Legal Institute, which seeks transparency into foreign funding flowing into Western academia. In an article titled "What Qatar Bought from Carnegie Mellon for $1 Billion," *The Free Press*—writing in the context of an antisemitism lawsuit against the university—detailed what Qatar receives in return for its massive funding, including potential compromises on academic freedom, curriculum influence, and the funding of key administrative positions such as the assistant vice provost for DEI and Title IX.[15] In 2025, the institute sued the Department of Education to receive records related to the Qatar Foundation's funding of Carnegie Mellon

---

13. Frannie Block and Maya Sulkin, "Qatar and China Are Pouring Billions Into Elite American Universities," *Free Press*, April 27, 2025, www.thefp.com/p/explosion-in-foreign-funding-for-american-universities.
14. U.S. Department of Education, "Section 117 Foreign Gift and Contract Public Transparency Dashboard," n.d., www.foreignfundinghighered.gov/.
15. Frannie Block, "What Qatar Bought from Carnegie Mellon for $1 Billion," *Free Press*, February 2, 2026, www.thefp.com/p/what-qatar-bought-for-1-billion.

University, Cornell University, Georgetown University, Harvard University, Northwestern University, and the University of Michigan.[16] The institute claimed that its lawsuit was due to the Department of Education's failure to respond to its request for various documents, including inquiries, reports, and memoranda concerning Qatar's involvement with several university programs, including Georgetown's campus in Doha and its Center for Contemporary Arab Studies in Washington, D.C.[17]

Qatar's influence, however, does not stop at Georgetown-Doha's campus. An investigative report by the *Middle East Forum* revealed that over the course of twenty years, Georgetown received more than $971 million from Qatari sources.[18] This funding has flowed not only to the Doha branch but also directly into the university's flagship campus in Washington, D.C. During this period, Georgetown's courses and research exhibited a growing ideological drift toward post-colonial scholarship, anti-Western critiques, and anti-Israel advocacy, with some faculty actively engaged in political activism related to the Israeli-Palestinian conflict or anti-Western interventionism in the Middle East. An illuminating Georgetown-specific example of the ideological fusion at the heart of the Leftist-Islamist alliance is the scholarship and teaching of Shenila Khoja Moolji, who in August 2022 was appointed as the Hamad bin Khalifa Al-Thani Endowed Chair of Muslim Societies at Georgetown University—a position named after Qatar's ruling emir and funded by the Qatari royal family. Her course "American Muslims" centers on

---

16. Judicial Watch, "Judicial Watch Sues Dept. of Education for Records on Funding of U.S. Universities' Operations in Qatar," *Judicial Watch*, January 29, 2025, www.judicialwatch.org/universities-operations-in-qatar/.

17. Ohad Merlin, "Watchdogs Sue US Government over Qatar's Billions in University Funding," *Jerusalem Post*, February 2, 2025, www.jpost.com/american-politics/article-840367.

18. Middle East Forum, "Qatar's Multidimensional Takeover of Georgetown University," January 20, 2026, www.meforum.org/mef-reports/qatars-multidimensional-takeover-of-georgetown-university.

how "Muslims in America hope to dismantle exploitative hierarchies" and examines "the role that religious ethics plays in this project"—language that unmistakably echoes Marxist calls to overthrow capitalist structures and challenge "systemic oppression."[19] Similarly, her course "Muslim Women and the West" sets out to counter the "racist, capitalist, and heteronormative logics" that supposedly shape the lives of Muslim women in Western societies.[20] These narratives combine classic Marxist critique (focusing on economics) with Gramscian cultural hegemony theory, positioning Western civilization as the "oppressor" despite the West offering significantly more freedoms than anywhere else in the "Muslim world."

The *Middle East Forum* report further noted that Qatari leadership—specifically Sheikh Abdulla bin Ali Al Thani, the son of the former Emir of Qatar Ali bin Abdullah Al Thani— enjoyed direct representation at the highest levels of Georgetown's Board of Directors, along with significant control over financial decisions that influence faculty hiring—creating clear risks of donor-driven bias in academic governance. As we saw in chapter 3, the phrase "He who pays the piper calls the tune" is applicable here, as Qatar's "soft power" in the form of financial donations allows the country to influence academic discourse, research, and curricula that align with the Leftist-Islamist agenda in the civil and political spheres.

Qatar's role in the ongoing "soft war" positions the small yet powerful country as a "king" on the metaphorical chessboard. This ultimate piece wields influence over other pieces, from the "pawns" on college campuses to the "rooks" in Congress. It orchestrates the game from a powerful position in which it is rarely, if ever, seen on the actual battlefield. As a key strategic underwriter of the Leftist-Islamist alliance, Qatar's financial strength, rather than its military capabilities, is its primary weapon. Its approach reminds us of Sun Tzu's strategy of winning a war

---

19. Ibid.
20. Ibid.

without direct military confrontation. It also uses another "nonviolent" weapon in its arsenal —an influential "voice box"—to amplify the Leftist-Islamist agenda around the world.

THE MICROPHONE OF "SOFT POWER": AL JAZEERA'S ROLE IN SHAPING "NARRATIVES"

Narrative control is a primary strategy for the Leftist-Islamist alliance. This non-direct maneuver to reframe public perception and cultivate "counterhegemony" echoes Orwell's *Nineteen Eighty-Four*, in which he stated, "Who controls the past controls the future; who controls the present controls the past." Just as the Inner Party ensured its media arm always aligned with its historical revisionism and propaganda, so, too, does Qatar, through its influential media arm, Al Jazeera, the state-funded news organization headquartered in Doha, Qatar's capital.

Founded in 1996, Al Jazeera originally focused on delivering Arabic-language news on current affairs to audiences in the Arab world, but it has since become the world's primary media platform for attacking the U.S.-Israel alliance. Its influence began to spread throughout the Middle East in the early 2000s, and by the start of the Arab Spring in 2010, it became a major catalyst for the revolts. To continue expanding its reach, the company initiated two key developments—Al Jazeera America (AJAM), which launched in 2013 but closed down in 2016 amid accusations of promoting "a strong bias for the Muslim Brotherhood," and AJ+, a social media platform launched in 2014 whose short-form videos on "social justice" issues are attractive to millennial audiences and Generation Z.[21] AJ+ describes itself in Marxist terms as providing

21. Hussein Ibish, "Why American Turned Off Al Jazeera," *New York Times*, February 17, 2016, www.nytimes.com/2016/02/18/opinion/why-america-turned-off-al-jazeera.html.

a "social justice lens on a world struggling for change." Critics say that it prioritizes "clickbait" and "sensational material," especially on issues related to the Israel-Palestine conflict.[22] These initiatives, and the outlet's ability to "control the narrative," are precisely where Qatar shapes global perspectives in ways that push the Leftist-Islamist agenda.

Another branch of Al Jazeera—Al Jazeera English, a 24-hour news channel launched in 2006—is one of the most vocal and influential media outlets in the world. Its coverage draws on critical race theory by consistently accusing Western countries of a "ubiquitous pattern of injustice and discrimination" against a variety of "victim groups," especially ethnic and religious minority populations in the West.[23] Regarding the Israel-Palestine conflict, academic studies and media analyses have shown how its "propaganda" amplifies Palestinian perspectives and dedicates more time and space to Palestinian voices than Israeli or Jewish voices, framing the conflict within the broader context of Israel's "occupation" of Palestinian territories. This Marxist-style oppressor-oppressed framing led Israel to ban Al Jazeera in May 2024 from operating within its borders, citing "incitement" and a lack of "impartiality." Like Israel, Egypt temporarily banned the Qatar-run news outlet in 2014 after three Al Jazeera journalists were imprisoned for allegedly spreading "fake news" and collaborating with the Muslim Brotherhood.[24] The Egyptian government blocked it again in 2017 for "supporting terrorism."[25]

---

22. HonestReporting, "Video: Is AJ+ Fake News?" March 15, 2017, honestreporting.com/video-is-aj-fake-news.
23. Lorenzo Vidino, "The Rise of 'Woke' Islamism in the West," Hudson Institute, January 23, 2022, www.hudson.org/node/44718.
24. India Tomorrow, "Egypt Court Bans Al Jazeera," *India Tomorrow*, September 3, 2014, indiatomorrow.net/2014/09/03/egypt-court-bans-al-jazeera/.
25. Reuters, "Egypt Blocks 21 Websites Including Al Jazeera—Security Sources," *Reuters*, May 24, 2017, www.reuters.com/article/markets/commodities/egypt-blocks-21-websites-including-al-jazeera-security-sources-idUSL8N1IQ758/.

Particularly troubling is the accusation that *Al Jazeera* embeds its journalists in Hamas. Anas al-Sharif, a prominent *Al Jazeera* journalist, was an active member of Hamas who received a salary from the group, serving as the head of a rocket-launching squad in Hamas' East Jabalia Battalion.[26] Another journalist, Abdallah Aljamal, who was platformed by *Al Jazeera* and was a spokesman for the Hamas-run labor ministry, held three October 7 hostages in his home with his family.[27] To be clear, Al-Sharif and Aljamal's cases are not an anomaly. Israeli-captured documents from Gaza indicate that six *Al Jazeera* journalists are or were members of either Hamas or Palestinian Islamic Jihad (PIJ), a designated terrorist organization by the United States, the United Kingdom, and the European Union.[28] In June 2025, an Israeli court affirmed the Israeli army's claim of a "close connection" between *Al Jazeera* and Hamas. The court noted that some *Al Jazeera* reporters in Gaza had become "assistants and partners" with Hamas and had even participated in terror attacks.

An important parallel exists here between the bans of *Al Jazeera* by countries like Israel and Egypt and the ban of the Muslim Brotherhood by Saudi Arabia and the United Arab Emirates. The parallel is that these Middle Eastern countries view the Muslim Brotherhood and *Al*

---

26. Emanuel Fabian and Times of Israel Staff, "IDF Says Gaza Documents Prove 6 Al Jazeera Journalists Are Hamas, PIJ Operatives," *Times of Israel*, October 23, 2024, www.timesofisrael.com/idf-says-gaza-documents-prove-6-al-jazeera-journalists-are-hamas-pij-operatives/.
27. Ronny Reyes, "Gaza Journalist Who Wrote for Al Jazeera Was Holding 3 Hostages in Home with Family, Israel Says," *New York Post*, June 9, 2024, nypost.com/2024/06/09/world-news/gaza-journalist-held-3-hostages-in-his-home-with-his-family-israeli-military-says/.
28. Ahmad Sharawi, "Captured Documents Show Al Jazeera Ties to Hamas, Islamic Jihad," Foundation for Defense of Democracies, October 29, 2024, www.fdd.org/analysis/policy_briefs/2024/10/29/captured-documents-show-al-jazeera-ties-to-hamas-islamic-jihad/.

Jazeera, whose operations are also banned by the Saudis and Emiratis, not just as political movements or news outlets, but also as ideological and political threats to their national stability and security. In both cases, these Middle Eastern countries have taken decisive action because they believe the Muslim Brotherhood and *Al Jazeera* are capable of inflicting chaos, a perspective that stands in contrast to their continued operation in Western nations. The U.A.E. government is wary enough of the Brotherhood's influence that it restricted government-funded scholarships for Emirati citizens to study at some universities in the United Kingdom, fearing that Emiratis would be radicalized and exposed to the group's influence on British campuses.[29] Austria is the only European country that has taken legal steps amounting to a ban on the Muslim Brotherhood. Following the 2020 Vienna terrorist attack, the Austrian parliament prohibited the dissemination, possession, and use of Muslim Brotherhood literature, slogans, and symbols.[30]

Returning to the U.S. domestic front, *Al Jazeera*'s content reveals support for Marxist movements on American soil and slanted, strongly left coverage aligned with the "progressive" movement discussed in previous chapters. A 2020 *Al Jazeera* opinion piece titled "Black Lives Matter and Lessons from Palestine" linked the BLM movement to the Palestinian struggle against Israeli "occupation," arguing that the experiences of African Americans and Palestinians are rooted in "anti-colonial" and "anti-racist" frameworks. This kind of framing is aimed at swaying public opinion and serving Qatar's strategic interests in furthering

29. "UAE Limiting Students Coming to UK over Muslim Brotherhood Concerns," *The Times*, January 9, 2026, www.thetimes.com/uk/education/article/uae-limiting-students-coming-to-uk-over-muslim-brotherhood-concerns-zvpdd6fqn.

30. Silvia Sardone, "Anti-Terror Law in Austria," Question E-oo3663/2021 to the Commission, European Parliament, July 20, 2021, www.europarl.europa.eu/doceo/document/E-9-2021-003663_EN.html.

Muslim Brotherhood narratives in American society. For these reasons, U.S. lawmakers have claimed that *Al Jazeera* should register as a foreign agent under the Foreign Agents Registration Act (FARA), which would require Qatar to disclose the nature of its political activities. Such a maneuver would provide further evidence that *Al Jazeera* is not simply offering "journalism" and "news" but promoting "deception" and "propaganda" on behalf of a foreign government.

My own encounters with *Al Jazeera* are useful for understanding how a nation can wield "soft power" by advancing "narratives" that align with the Leftist-Islamist agenda. Following the 2020 success of my *Newsweek* article, which applied the teachings of Muhammad as documented in the hadith traditions to the early COVID-19 pandemic, *Al Jazeera Arabic*, the company's flagship program, hosted me for a substantial ten-minute segment to discuss Muhammad's life and legacy as well as "Islamophobia."[31] During this interview, one of the two anchors of the show expressed bafflement that I was not Muslim and encouraged my conversion live on air.[32] This experience of urging conversion, which often surfaced in my previous work on Muhammad, highlights *Al Jazeera*'s subtle form of coercion and measurement of a person's worth not by their morals or values, but by their political beliefs and religious identity—a dogmatic approach characteristic of the ideological purity sought by the Leftist-Islamist convergence. Two months later, *Al Jazeera Balkans*, another important component of *Al Jazeera*'s media arm, featured

31. Craig Considine, "Can the Power of Prayer Alone Stop a Pandemic like the Coronavirus? Even the Prophet Muhammad Thought Otherwise," *Newsweek*, March 17, 2020, www.newsweek.com/prophet-prayer-muhammad-covid-19-coronavirus-1492798.

32. Al Jazeera Arabic, "Prophet Muhammad, COVID-19, and Islamophobia—Dr. Craig Considine on Al Jazeera," YouTube, video dated June 15, 2020, www.youtube.com/watch?v=eaJOLk3P1es

me in an even longer twenty-five-minute segment on a range of topics.[33] While these appearances suggested a favorable reception of my views, my later vocal defense of the Abraham Accords and Israel following October 7 led to a complete cessation of invitations from the company. This abrupt shift, I contend, underscores *Al Jazeera*'s desire and ability to squash voices that threaten the Leftist-Islamist alliance. Qatar's media giant is not only able to "control the narrative," but it can also turn narratives "on" and "off" like a faucet that controls the flow of water.

Two decades have passed since its founding, and *Al Jazeera*'s global profile has only grown, particularly in its ability to control narratives surrounding the Israeli-Palestinian conflict. This media dominance allows it to function as a powerful amplifier for the Leftist-Islamist alliance, shaping global public opinion by consistently presenting a one-sided, Manichaean-like narrative that demonizes Israel and implicitly supports anti-Western sentiments. A "sound strategy" in the "soft war" is ensuring that it registers under FARA in the U.S. and its equivalent policies in Western countries.

IRAN'S "AXIS OF RESISTANCE": THE GEOPOLITICAL BATTLE WITH THE "GREAT SATAN"

The Manichaean worldview, which divides the world into forces of "good" and "evil," is a defining characteristic of the radical ideologies unpacked in this book. Like those ideologies, it is attractive to many not only for its simplicity but also for its moral certainty. In an earlier stage of my professional development, I myself was drawn to its framing, which made thinking about the world and all its complexity quite easy, as seen in the work of figures like political activist and critic Noam Chomsky. In 2008,

33. Al Jazeera Balkans, "Recite Al Jazeeri—Craig Considine," YouTube, video dated July 31, 2020, www.youtube.com/watch?v=VA8P4zwgV-4&t=3s.

I filmed him in an interview with Akbar Ahmed, a scholar of Islam and promoter of interfaith dialogue. In it, Chomsky claimed that American national identity was rooted in "myth" and "fear," a framing that at the time aligned with my then nascent disdain for the United States due to the wars in Afghanistan and Iraq. Following the interview, I read several of Chomsky's books, including *Hegemony or Survival: America's Quest for Global Dominance* and *Failed States: The Abuse of Power and the Assault on Democracy*, which only furthered my contempt. These books sent me down the Chomsky "rabbit hole," in which I viewed him as an authoritative intellectual whose critiques of America were well-founded. However, as my knowledge grew over the years and my perspective became more nuanced, I gradually grew apart from Chomsky's positions and the Leftist-Islamist alliance. While I still acknowledge some validity in his historical and modern criticism of U.S. foreign policy, I now recognize the "radicalism" inherent in his stances, which are ideologically predetermined and in which all evidence and context are filtered through a Manichaean lens.

Chomsky's radicalism, as Horowitz described it, is "shaped by one overriding imperative—to demonize America as the fount of worldly evil."[34] He added that the Left is under the spell of the "Chomsky phenomenon," which he described as:

> . . . the expression of an anti-American cult, for whose primitive hatred Chomsky performs a ventriloquist function. Chomsky did not spring into being *de novo*, but it is the product of a left-wing culture that had already traveled far down the path of fanaticism and the conviction that a nation conceived in liberty and dedicated to the proposition that all men are created equal is really a Great Satan—an empire built on slavery and dedicated to oppression and imperial conquest.[35]

---

34. Horowitz, *Unholy Alliance*, 95.
35. Ibid., 101.

The "Chomsky phenomenon," which recalls Orwell's warnings of inverting reality, mirrors the rhetoric emanating from Iran, whose leaders have for decades stood for "Death to America" and "Death to Israel." For both Chomsky and Iranian leaders, America is the "Great Satan," the primary force responsible for all the injustices afflicting the modern world, and Israel is the "Little Satan" operating as a "Western colony" in the Middle East. Their views are fueled by the Manichaean and Marxist worldview that paints America as "evil," the ultimate "oppressor," and a country on the "wrong side of history."

As the archenemy of the U.S.-Israel alliance, Iran is positioned as another "king" on the metaphorical chessboard. Its foreign policy is rooted in opposing both American influence and Israel's existence in the Middle East. The country often frames itself as the head of the "axis of resistance" to Western dominance by providing financial, military, and political support to a network of state and nonstate actors that are actively hostile to the West. Iran's multifaceted strategy has been executed through numerous regional maneuvers in the West on the Middle East battlefield. It is the world's largest state sponsor of Hamas, providing it with significant funding and military support to boost its operations, particularly the construction of Hamas's tunnel network in Gaza.[36] Iran is also the primary benefactor of Hezbollah, the Shia terrorist group in Lebanon, providing it with advanced weaponry, funding, and training in its war with Israel.[37] The Houthis of Yemen, another foe of the West, also receive missiles, drones, and technical expertise from Iranian leaders.[38] In Western countries, Tehran has visible outposts in mosques that, at

36. Thomas Clayton, "Iran-Supported Groups in the Middle East and U.S. Policy," Congressional Research Service, September 26, 2024, www.congress.gov/crs-product/IF12587.

37. Ibid.

38. Ibid.

face value, serve as places of worship, but in reality they serve instead as a platform for projecting Iran's revolutionary ideology, influence, and recruitment abroad.[39] The Islamic Centre of England, for example, has for years displayed messages from Iran's late Supreme Leader, Ali Khamenei, effectively relaying official state messaging to a British audience that included children and youth.[40] A recent 100-page report authored by John Woodcock (Lord Walney), a member of the House of Lords with whom I conversed at the 2025 Middle East Forum conference in Washington, D.C., described Iran's systematic exploitation of the U.K. Charity sector, alleging that Tehran-linked organizations have been used to spread regime-aligned narratives, build influence networks, channel funding through opaque means, and encourage agitation and division within communities.[41] Iran is clearly a strategic kingpin for the "axis of resistance," posing a direct military challenge to Western civilization and its effort to maintain regional stability in the Middle East.

In addition to its direct financial and military assistance to nonstate actors, Iran provides "moral support" and "solidarity" to the "foot soldiers" of the Leftist-Islamist alliance. In 2024, Ali Khamenei, the head of the Iranian government, wrote a letter to American university students who were protesting in support of Palestine. Part of his letter read:

> This is a message of empathy and solidarity from us in the Islamic world to you. As you have been part of the Resistance Front, a branch of the Resistance Front has also begun a new life in the United States.
>
> It is with great pleasure that I have been following the honorable struggle of your students in American universities in support of the

39. Potkin Azarmehr, "They Laugh at the U.K. While the Watchdogs Sleep," *Middle East Forum* (MEF Online), April 8, 2026, www.meforum.org/mef-online/they-laugh-at-the-uk-while-the-watchdogs-sleep.
40. Ibid.
41. Ibid.

> oppressed people of Palestine. Your actions have created a wave of empathy and support for the Palestinians across the world.
>
> The American government, and the Western governments that support it, are openly supporting the usurper and brutal Zionist regime. However, you, the students, have stood up against this. Your brave resistance and honorable stance against the brutal regime and its supporters are a great source of hope for us.
>
> I advise you to become familiar with the Qur'an and the teachings of Islam. The Qur'an has a very clear message about justice and resistance against oppression.
>
> The future is yours. It is up to you to build a new world free from injustice and tyranny. Do not let false narratives of the media deceive you. Become a voice of truth and justice.[42]

Khamenei's letter exemplifies the "soft power" strategy, which uses nonmilitary and ideological methods to achieve its aims on the battlefield. Addressing the students as a "Resistance Front," a narrative that creates a sense of shared purpose with Iran's agenda, turned an American protest movement into an international coalition against "imperialism," one that favors Islamist principles over Western principles. There is also irony in the letter, highlighted by the contrast between the freedom of speech enjoyed by these students in America and the highly controlled environment of Iran, where such dissent and displays of "public protest" are swiftly—and often brutally—suppressed by Iran's authoritarian regime.

---

42. The Office of the Supreme Leader, "Dear Young Students in America, You Now Stand on the Right Side of History," The Office of the Supreme Leader, May 30, 2024, www.leader.ir/en/content/27338/Leader-s-Letter-to-American-University-Students-with-a-Conscience.

College students in the United States responded in like fashion following the U.S. government's decision to bomb the nuclear facilities in Iran. The National Students for Justice in Palestine (NSJP) issued an Instagram post, writing:

> The empire will fall, from Gaza to Tehran. The unprovoked attacks the U.S. and the Zionist entity have launched against Iran prove only one thing—imperialism in the region will not stop at suffocating Palestine. From Iraq to Lebanon, Libya, Yemen, Syria, and now Iran, the Empire [sic] demands constant expansion and destabilization. . . . We must be clear—Nuclear development is neither a crime nor the reason for the U.S.' war against Iran. The U.S. Empire cannot permit the continued existence of a country that dares to stand against Zionism and imperialism.[43]

SJP splinter groups across higher education rallied to share NSJP's post. Faculty for Justice in Palestine (FJP) chapters at the University of California–Berkeley and the University of Florida reposted it to their Instagram stories.[44] At Columbia University, Unity Fields, a radical far-left group based in the United States, posted a photograph of the coffins of fallen American soldiers, captioning it, "Soon, Inshallah [God willing]."[45] Responding to the post, Asaf Romirowsky, a Middle East expert, blamed left-wing academics—the "bishops" on the chessboard—for NSJP's positions,[46] as detailed in chapter two. Another expert, Alex Joffe, raised the alarm on the post because it suggested "nearly complete

---

43. Dion J. Pierre, "Pro-Hamas Campus Groups Call for Toppling US Government, Killing Soldiers," *Algemeiner*, June 23, 2025, www.algemeiner.com/2025/06/23/pro-hamas-campus-groups-call-toppling-us-government-killing-soldiers/.
44. Ibid.
45. Ibid.
46. Ibid.

overlap in interests and even personnel" with other Leftist and Islamist action-oriented groups, such as the Party for Socialism and Liberation, the Democratic Socialists of America, and Code Pink.[47]

Iran's current role as "kingpin" of the Leftist-Islamist alliance finds its roots in the 1979 Iranian Revolution, a critical moment that initially united Leftists and Islamists in opposition to the "Western-backed regime" of Mohammad Reza Pahlavi, Iran's former monarch, who, the revolutionaries claimed, was an American "puppet," too "Westernized," and not "Islamic" enough. Pahlavi's opponent, Ayatollah Ruhollah Musavi Khomeini, the commander of the Islamist faction, emerged as the primary figure of "resistance" to the Western-backed monarchical ruler, with bashing the U.S.-Israel alliance at the forefront of his rhetoric and agenda. Khomeini successfully mobilized Leftist allies and fellow Islamists in a fragile but well-organized and effective movement based on Third Worldism, the Marxist ideology of the Cold War that centered "marginalization," "oppression," and "hegemony" in its strategy. The alliance, however, was short-lived. Not long after seizing power, the Islamists, who were working toward an "Islamic state," cut off relations with Leftists, who were advocating for a "secular state." The Islamists ended up consolidating power, implementing Sharia, and suppressing human rights, most notably freedom of dissent, freedom of expression, and freedom of speech, all of which are still absent in Iran today. This breakdown in relations suggests that the current Leftist-Islamist alliance could be short-lived, with "hegemonic" Islamist forces eventually "pulling the plug" on the "foot soldiers" (the "pawns"), who may be deemed no longer strategically useful to the Islamist cause in the long run.

In the immediate future, it is unlikely that their political agendas will shift considerably due to their fierce opposition to the West and

47. Ibid.

their allegiance to Marxism, an ideology championed years before the Iranian Revolution in communist China.

ECHOES OF THE RED GUARD: MAO'S LEGACY IN "CULTURAL MARXISM"

Once unleashed, the power of "revolutionary" ideologies like that of Iran in 1979 can cast a long shadow in any war, whether "soft" or "hard." An illustration of this claim is found in the "Cultural Revolution," the Chinese upheaval initiated by Mao Zedong, the former communist dictator of China, whose legacy and strategy are reflected in today's "soft war" battlefields.

The "Great Proletarian Cultural Revolution," as it was officially named, drew on both "classical Marxism" (class struggle) and "cultural Marxism" (cultural transformation). Beginning in May 1966 and ending in 1976, the revolution plunged China into political, social, and economic chaos, as communist regimes typically do. The movement was driven by the "Red Guard," a paramilitary organization and mass movement of primarily university students, Mao's very own "foot soldiers."[48] Per his order, these students were tasked with destroying the "Four Olds": "Old Ideas," "Old Culture," "Old Customs," and "Old Habits."[49] These tasks remind us of Orwell's warning that communist governments create "new narratives" to assert control and purge the "Inner Party" of ideological "revisionists," a tactic which we have seen repeatedly in this book.

The "Red Terror" movement had a tactical playbook called the "Lit-

---

48. Britannica Encyclopedia, "Red Guards," *Britannica Encyclopedia*, n.d., www.britannica.com/topic/Red-Guards.

49. Tillman Durdin, "China Transformed by Elimination of 'Four Olds,'" *New York Times*, May 19, 1971, www.nytimes.com/1971/05/19/archives/china-transformed-by-elimination-of-four-olds.html.

tle Red Book."[50] This pocket-sized collection of Mao's quotations and teachings was designed to advance communist doctrine and inspire the zealous and youthful "foot soldiers" in their revolutionary mission. Its Marxist-like slogans and calls for "self-sacrifice" mirror contemporary calls for "martyrdom" within the Leftist-Islamist alliance, whose factions have publicly declared their commitment to winning the "soft war" by "any means necessary." By "Red August" of 1966, Mao's "foot soldiers" had formed divisions in classrooms across the country to transform the "old culture" from within, a Gramscian strategy to change China by operating in the civil sphere.[51] Red Guard gangs, with red armbands denoting their ideological allegiance to Mao, roamed cities like Beijing and Shanghai, targeting anyone deemed "elite," "intellectual," or "too Western."[52] The "foot soldiers" also behaved in ways similar to today's Leftists and Islamists by engaging in "struggle sessions," where they publicly humiliated—and sometimes killed—the perceived enemies of the revolution.

Equipped with their "Little Red Book," the Red Guard inflicted widespread chaos in Chinese society. Approximately 1,800 people lost their lives in Beijing in August and September 1966 alone. By late 1968, even Mao recognized his "Cultural Revolution" had spiraled out of control.[53] In a calculated maneuver to assert his dominance, he issued instructions to send millions of urban youths to countryside camps for "reeducation"—a testament to his understanding that "information war-

---

50. BBC News, "Who, What, Why—What Is the Little Red Book?" *BBC News*, November 26, 2015, www.bbc.com/news/magazine-34932800.

51. Tom Phillips, "The Cultural Revolution—All You Need to Know about China's Political Convulsion," *Guardian*, May 10, 2016, www.theguardian.com/world/2016/may/11/the-cultural-revolution-50-years-on-all-you-need-to-know-about-chinas-political-convulsion.

52. Ibid.

53. Ibid.

fare," "propaganda," and "ideological training" are critical to achieving the "revolution."[54] At least one expert has estimated that 1.7 million people died because of the Cultural Revolution.[55]

Maoism's convergence with the Leftist-Islamist agenda has roots in the Palestinian nationalist movements of the 1960s. In 1965, a delegation of the Palestine Liberation Organization (PLO) traveled to China to meet with Mao, who, during the meeting, sympathized with the Palestinian "resistance" movement by claiming that "Imperialism is afraid of China and of the Arabs" and that Israel and Taiwan are "bases of [Western] imperialism in Asia."[56] He added, "[Palestinians] are the gate of the great continent and [the Chinese] are the rear," suggesting that both Palestine and China are at the edges of the global "anti-imperialist" movement.[57] Following this 1965 meeting, Mao proceeded to arm Palestinian militants with substantial quantities of weapons and ammunition. The Palestinian national charter at that time included a Maoist-style statement: "Armed struggle is the only way to liberate Palestine." It also stated that "liberation" through "violence" is the "overall strategy, not merely a tactical phase."[58] Meanwhile, the Popular Front

---

54. Yihong Pan, "From Red Guards to Thinking Individuals—China's Youth in the Cultural Revolution," *Asian in World History: The Twentieth Century* 14, no. 3 (Winter 2009), www.asianstudies.org/publications/eaa/archives/from-red-guards-to-thinking-individuals-chinas-youth-in-the-cultural-revolution/.

55. Melissa De Witte, "China's Cultural Revolution Was a Power Grab from within the Government, Not from Without, Stanford Sociologist Finds," *Stanford Report*, October 29, 2019, news.stanford.edu/stories/2019/10/violence-unfolded-chinas-cultural-revolution.

56. Benjamin R. Young, "How Chinese Maoism Intellectually Shaped Modern Palestinian Jihadism," *Diplomat*, May 16, 2024, thediplomat.com/2024/05/how-chinese-maoism-intellectually-shaped-modern-palestinian-jihadism/.

57. Ibid.

58. The Avalon Project, "The Palestinian National Charter—Resolutions of the Palestine National Council July 1–17, 1968," Yale Law School, Lillian Gold-

for the Liberation of Palestine (PFLP), a designated terrorist group, adopted Mao's strategy of a "People's War" and "armed struggle" following Egypt, Jordan, and Syria's defeat against Israel in the 1967 Six-Day War, and George Habash, the PFLP founder, went so far as to say, "Our best friend, in fact, is China."[59] Similarly, in 1970, the leader of the Palestine Liberation Organization, Yasser Arafat, declared Mao and China to be the "biggest influence in supporting our revolution and strengthening its perseverance."[60]

Mao's death in 1976 led to the decline of China's direct involvement with the Palestinian cause. This void, however, was filled in 1979 by the Iranian Revolution, which, as previously discussed, provided a source of inspiration for Marxists and jihadists across the Middle East. The Iranian Revolution used jihad to align with Mao's vision of "armed struggle" and "righteous justice," and, like Mao, Khomeini "recruited" students and activists—the "foot soldiers" on the metaphorical battlefield—to execute the "revolution."

This historical convergence of Maoism and the Palestinian cause shows how Leftist revolutionary strategies are tied to Islamist goals of challenging Western hegemony. Given this historical legacy, it should be unsurprising to readers that China-linked entities today, such as the People's Forum and TikTok, which I turn to later in this chapter, are allies to Hamas and other Palestinian groups. These entities are defending the Palestinian "gate" in Gaza, to borrow Mao's metaphor, as well as the Chinese "rear." Yet, there is a deafening silence among the "foot soldiers" in their refusal to condemn China. After all, condemning the

---

man Law Library, n.d., avalon.law.yale.edu/20th_century/plocov.asp.

59. Oriana Fallaci, "A Leader of the Fedayeen—We Want a War Like the Vietnamese War," *Life Magazine*, June 1970, 35.

60. Charles Xu, "The Gates of the Great Continent—Palestine, China, and the War for Humanity's Future (Part 1)," *MRonline*, March 11, 2024, mronline.org/2024/03/11/the-gates-of-the-great-continent/.

CCP would be akin to attacking their own ally, a maneuver that would undermine the alliance's entire operational strategy.

MAO'S SHADOW: THE UYGHUR GENOCIDE AND "SELECTIVE OUTRAGE"

A clear double standard exhibited by the Leftist-Islamist alliance is its silence surrounding China's reported "genocide" of the Uyghurs, a transnational ethnic Turkic and predominantly Sunni Muslim group with a significant population in Xinjiang, a western province in China. The Leftist-Islamist alliance relies on "selective outrage" to create "narratives" surrounding certain conflicts while deliberately obscuring or even ignoring others. This collective indifference of the alliance to the plight of the Uyghurs exposes the alliance's selective engagement based on geopolitical convenience rather than on consistent moral principles.

The Uyghurs have been subjected to a program reminiscent of the "Cultural Revolution." The U.S. State Department, under both Republican[61] and Democratic[62] presidents, has accused the CCP of creating and maintaining "reeducation camps," wherein Uyghurs are "reprogrammed" to be "more Chinese" and "less Uyghur." Inside these camps, Uyghurs have been subjected to abuses, mutilation, torture, and even "disappearances," with individuals vanishing into what are modern-day Chinese gulags.[63]

---

61. Michael R. Pompeo, "Determination of the Secretary of State on Atrocities in Xinjiang," U.S. Department of State, January 19, 2021, 2017-2021.state.gov/determination-of-the-secretary-of-state-on-atrocities-in-xinjiang/.

62. BBC News, "US—China 'Committed Genocide Against Uighurs,'" *BBC News*, January 20, 2021, www.bbc.com/news/world-us-canada-55723522.

63. U.S. Department of State, "The Chinese Communist Party's Human Rights Abuses in Xinjiang," U.S. Department of State, n.d., 2017-2021.state.

One "vanished" Uyghur—Gulshan Abbas, a retired medical doctor—became a symbol of the CCP's treatment of the Uyghurs when she was forcibly detained on September 11, 2018. A week earlier, Gulshan's sister, Rushan Abbas, a Uyghur advocate, had given a talk at the Hudson Institute, a conservative think tank based in Washington, D.C., in which she publicly condemned the CCP, suggesting that Gulshan's imprisonment was a direct result of her sister's advocacy. In March 2019, Gulshan was reportedly sentenced to twenty years in prison and eventually convicted of "participating in a terrorist organization," "aiding terrorist activities," and "gathering a crowd to disrupt social order."[64] These are tactics reminiscent of scenes in Orwell's *Nineteen Eighty-Four*, where an authoritarian regime creates a "false narrative" to achieve its own self-serving goals.

Rushan's work inspired me to host her at Rice University in November 2021.[65] Gulshan, at that time, had been missing for three years, with no information on her whereabouts despite efforts to find her.[66] At Rice, Rushan shared testimonies from Uyghurs in the "reeducation camps," detailing forced marriages, organ harvesting, coerced abandonment of ethnic and religious identities, mass rape, and forced labor. Given the state of these affairs, it is ironic that Leftists and Islamists—the self-proclaimed "champions" of the "oppressed"—remain silent on Gulshan and the broader Uyghur genocide, focusing their efforts instead on "freeing

---

gov/ccpabuses/.

64. United States Commission on International Religious Freedom, "Gulshan Abbas," n.d., www.uscirf.gov/religious-prisoners-conscience/forb-victims-database/gulshan-abbas.

65. Amy McCaig, "Rice Talk to Focus on Uyghur Genocide in China," *Rice University News and Media Relations*, November 1, 2021, news.rice.edu/news/2021/rice-talk-focus-uyghur-genocide-china.

66. Hajera Naveed, "Uyghur Activist Speaks at Rice on Genocide in Xinjiang," *Rice Thresher*, November 9, 2021, www.ricethresher.org/article/2021/11/uyghur-activist-speaks-at-rice-on-genocide-in-xinjiang.

Palestine" and defending Hamas's "martyrs." One wonders: are the Uyghurs simply not an "acceptable" marginalized community because their suffering implicates the CCP, a regime that certain elements within the Leftist-Islamist alliance find strategically advantageous to protect? Or is the lack of outrage over documented human rights abuses due to the "absence" of U.S. or Israeli involvement in the matter? Indeed, perhaps the saying, "No Jews, No News," is applicable to this curious predicament, given that Jewish people and Israel are not directly involved in the Uyghur plight in Xinjiang, and therefore, the Uyghur plight is thus a "non-issue" for many groups within the Leftist-Islamist alliance. Regardless of one's answer to these questions, the general silence is a testament to the alliance's strategic alignment with authoritarian powers, even when those powers commit atrocities against Muslim populations that are primarily categorized by the Leftist-Islamist alliance as an "oppressed" population.

Reflecting on the metaphorical chessboard, every silence and every move made by the Leftist-Islamist alliance is a calculation of power, not of principle. Its strategic silence on the Uyghur genocide reveals a moral compromise. The alliance's selective indignation transforms human rights into a tactical instrument, a piece to be moved or ignored depending on the desired outcome in the war against the U.S.-Israel alliance in particular and the West more broadly. Unfortunately, the Leftist-Islamist alliance has prioritized strategic advantage over moral clarity. This cold calculus of power, however, is not new. It is a strategy with historical roots in the rise of communist ideologies in the twentieth century.

WEAPONIZING ALGORITHMS: TIKTOK AS A MODERN-DAY TROJAN HORSE

The rise of communism in Russia in 1917, which took Czar Nicholas II and his Romanov family dynasty by surprise, led to the rise of the Soviet

Union and the Cold War. The Russian czar failed to recognize the ideological battles being waged in Russian classrooms, at coffee houses, and on city streets. This misstep, which eventually led to the murder of the Romanov family at the hands of the communist Bolsheviks, is an important analogy for another insidious realm used by the Leftist-Islamist alliance—the digital battlefield—where "silent weapons" are used on the front lines of the "soft war." Ringing true in this case is the age-old military axiom, "Capture the minds of the young, and you capture the future of a nation."

TikTok, the social media platform that used to be fully owned and controlled by ByteDance, a Chinese company headquartered in Beijing, has emerged as a powerful piece on the metaphorical chessboard and a key "king" on digital battlefields. Critics claim that this social media entity has surpassed "the resonance of weapons" and delineated "a global divide" on the Israel-Palestine issue.[67] TikTok has been accused of being a CCP propaganda tool, a claim backed by a 2024 *Forbes* report revealing that the CCP has the ability to access and exploit TikTok's data at any time.[68] With more than 150 million American users, just under half the country's population, TikTok is not a "neutral" app, but a strategically engineered mechanism for ideological indoctrination. Its users are, in fact, being targeted by a specific agenda designed to attack America and Israel both internally and externally. These developments raised national security concerns and led to the Protecting Americans from Foreign Adversary Controlled Applications ACT (PAFACAA), which specifically

---

67. Mostafa Ahmed, "The War on TikTok—Security Concerns and Anti-Semitism," Al Habtoor Research Centre, April 22, 2024, www.habtoorresearch.com/programmes/the-war-on-tiktok-security-concerns-and-anti-semitism/.
68. Emily Baker-White, "Congress Wants Answers about the FBI and DOJ's TikTok Investigation," *Forbes*, December 7, 2023, www.forbes.com/sites/emily-baker-white/2023/12/07/congress-wants-answers-about-fbi-doj-tiktok-investigation/?sh=4f8d0b4278df.

targeted apps like TikTok, deeming them "foreign adversary–controlled applications" by the Chinese government. PAFACAA required ByteDance to divest TikTok's U.S. operations, which led to the 2026 formation of TikTok USDS Joint Venture LLC, a U.S.-based entity to operate the application domestically. The restructuring of TikTok, which gave ByteDance a 19.9% minority stake in the LLC, aimed to address security concerns surrounding content moderation and algorithm retraining, but its partial ownership still enables veiled influence to permeate American digital spaces, perpetuating the "soft war" through narrative shaping and algorithmic manipulation.

George Orwell, again, is a relevant theorist in understanding the dynamics involved in the digital battlefields of the "soft war." His writings on propaganda, where the Inner Party uses a controlled narrative to manipulate a population, can be compared to TikTok's algorithms, a hidden mechanism to control narratives. American venture capitalist Jeff Morris Jr. highlighted the power of TikTok's algorithm in a series of X posts after he engaged with one post supporting the Palestinian cause. Subsequently, Morris's entire feed "became aggressively anti-Israel," as if he were being "told to see this war with Israel being the evil side."[69] He claimed that because the TikTok narrative is now so anti-Israel, "the engagement flywheel" encourages creators to support the pro-Palestinian narrative "because it is getting the most attention, and creating anti-Israel content helps them increase their following." This reality creates an endless feedback loop where a specific worldview is not just presented but also algorithmically enforced. In this context, TikTok is a tool of Orwellian manipulation, in which reality is inverted to suit a predetermined political agenda.

---

69. Erin Hale, "TikTok Faces Calls for Ban amid Claims of Anti-Israel 'Indoctrination,'" *Al Jazeera*, November 10, 2023, www.aljazeera.com/news/2023/11/10/tiktok-faces-renewed-calls-for-a-ban-amid-pro-hamas-anti-israel-claims.

TikTok entered the political spotlight in the immediate aftermath of October 7, amid claims that its algorithms were pushing young people to support pro-Hamas and anti-Jewish content. Senator Josh Hawley of Missouri, in a letter critical of TikTok's ability to "brainwash" young Americans, cited a Harvard CAPS-Harris Poll in which 51 percent of Americans aged 18–24 said Hamas's attacks were justified by "Palestinian grievances," a view that stood in contrast to older Americans and non-TikTok users, who overwhelmingly back Israel.[70] Similarly, then Senator Marco Rubio of Florida stated after October 7 that TikTok, among other social media platforms, had become "cesspools of [pro-Hamas] misinformation and indoctrination."[71] Senator James E. Risch of Idaho, the top Republican on the Senate Foreign Affairs Committee, shared his views in a letter to the Federal Trade Commission in which he declared, "TikTok is built like an indoctrination machine and its user base is comprised of one of the most impressionable and vulnerable populations—children."[72] These criticisms are supported by an internal memo written by Israeli employees of TikTok, who revealed that the company had rejected ads from the families of Israeli hostages as "too political" while accepting ones from pro-Palestinian groups. The Israeli employees of TikTok also claimed that "American users are BOMBARDED with paid ads that present the misery of children in Gaza," but are kept from seeing anything similar about Israeli hostages taken by Hamas.[73] These policies led TikTok's top lobbyist in Israel,

70. Ibid.

71. Ibid.

72. Fox News, "China Using TikTok as 'Indoctrination Machine' Against America's Youth, GOP Senator Warns," *Fox News*, July 31, 2023, www.risch.senate.gov/public/index.cfm/2023/7/china-using-tiktok-as-indoctrination-machine-against-america-s-youth-gop-senator-warns.

73. Cole S. Aronson, "Israel's TikTok Problem," *Jewish Review of Books*, March 13, 2024, jewishreviewofbooks.com/foreign-policy/15881/israels-tiktok-problem/.

Barak Herscowitz, to resign in protest in 2024, although TikTok claims that he was fired as part of a "strategic shift" in the company's approach to "public policy leadership."[74]

In another public controversy amid the heat of the Israel-Hamas war, TikTok gained widespread attention after users began virally sharing a 2002 letter from Osama bin Laden, the al-Qaeda operative responsible for the September 11, 2001, attacks that killed nearly three thousand Americans. Bin Laden's letter criticized U.S. support for Israel, condemned America's presence in the Middle East, and issued an array of antisemitic slurs. Though TikTok announced it eventually prohibited the letter for violating its rules on supporting terrorism, the letter had already gone viral. In response, lawmakers renewed calls for the app's ban, accusing it of promoting "pro-terrorist" propaganda to influence Americans.[75] This incident underscored how the "soft war" operates in the digital sphere. Narratives are not just formed online, but are also actively distributed, amplified, or squashed by entities whose operations are carefully monitored by authoritarian regimes.

The CCP's influence over TikTok allows it—a "king"—to engage in the "soft war" from a distance, recalling Sun Tzu's emphasis on indirect and nonviolent conflict. The app effectively behaves like Orwell's Ministry of Truth, with its agenda of controlling the narrative to shape not just the current "reality" but also the future. These realities remind us that freedom is not free and the price for it is not merely internal vigilance, but also external vigilance, which today extends beyond Western borders into digital spaces.

---

74. Ibid.

75. Sheila Dang and David Shepardson, "TikTok to Prohibit Videos Promoting Bin Laden's 'Letter to America,'" *Reuters*, November 16, 2023, www.reuters.com/world/middle-east/tiktok-prohibit-videos-promoting-bin-ladens-letter-america-2023-11-16/.

SHIFTING ALLIANCES: TRANSNATIONAL MOVEMENTS AND MY POSITION ON THE CHESSBOARD

Building on my analysis of the role that militant groups and countries play within the Leftist-Islamist alliance, my focus now shifts to two transnational movements that are active on "soft war" battlefields and with which I had direct encounters over the years. My close relationships with them highlight a critical fact: alliances are not static in the "soft war," as we saw with the Leftist-Islamist split following the Iranian and Bolshevik revolutions. These two transnational entities—the Gülen movement and the Ahmadiyya community—are both Islam-oriented with a presence in dozens of countries around the world, making them significant "kings" on the hypothetical chessboard.

My own position on the chessboard has been shaped by the Gülen movement, a primarily Turkey-centered social and religious network advocating for education, interfaith dialogue, and community service in the civil sphere. My first contact with the movement, also known by the Turkish term *Hizmet*, occurred when I accepted my job at Rice University in 2015. While teaching a course titled "Muslims in American Society," I organized a "field trip" for my students to the Raindrop Turkish House in Houston. We were met with excellent hospitality, genuine commitment to dialogue, and a tour through a grand ballroom, various cultural rooms, classrooms, a restaurant, and an impressive prayer space named after Istanbul's famous Blue Mosque. It was a positive experience. I admired the community's dedication to interfaith initiatives and civic service, seeing them as both spiritually enlightened Muslims and productive members of society who sought to contribute to the betterment of the West.

That initial 2015 visit sparked a relationship that thrived for years. Dozens of *Hizmet* centers around the United States, from Las Vegas to Baton Rouge to Washington, D.C., invited me to their towns and cities to give talks and spend time with their community members. My speaking engagements at their cultural centers and mosques included lectures at universities, meetings with students at Gülen charter schools, and more intimate sessions inside people's homes. These opportunities were created after I published my book, *The Humanity of Muhammad: A Christian View*, with one of Hizmet's publishing arms, Blue Dome Press.[76] The book was warmly received and was the reason that I nearly met Fethullah Gülen, the Islamic philosopher, author, and founder of the movement, at his remote estate in the Pocono Mountains in Pennsylvania. Unfortunately, he was ill at the time I visited the estate, so I did not meet him, but my trip there introduced me to other key figures in the movement. Enes Kanter Freedom, the former NBA player and a close companion of Gülen's, became my friend. I hosted him for an event at Rice in 2023, where he spoke about his advocacy for the plight of the Uyghurs and his opposition to authoritarian regimes around the world. Enes, in turn, invited me to help him with his initiative, the Abrahamic Athletic Academy, a youth program designed to use basketball to build bridges and train the next generation of leaders in interfaith dialogue and people-to-people diplomacy. To my knowledge, that program never manifested, and my line of communication with both Enes and the Gülen movement since October 7 has become virtually nonexistent.

The Gülen movement is caught up in Muslim Brotherhood–related issues within Turkey. Following the failed Turkish coup in 2016, President Recep Tayyip Erdoğan, an advocate of the Brotherhood and a former Gülen ally, launched a sweeping campaign against the movement, declaring it a "foreign terrorist organization" (FETO) and blaming its leaders for the attempted overthrow.[77] A massive crackdown com-

76. Craig Considine, *The Humanity of Muhammad—A Christian View* (Clifton, N.J.: Blue Dome Press, 2020).

77. "Turkey Officially Designates Gulen Religious Group as Terrorists," *Reuters*, May 31, 2016, www.reuters.com/article/world/turkey-officially-desig-

menced, resulting in the detention and imprisonment of hundreds of thousands of Gülen-affiliated citizens, with many more forced to flee the country. Erdoğan's attack was multifaceted, employing both "hard power" through detentions and purges, and "soft power" to control the narrative by using state-controlled media to reshape public opinion on Hizmet. He also unsuccessfully lobbied Congress to designate the Gülen movement a "terrorist organization."

Given Erdoğan's close ties to the Muslim Brotherhood and Islamism in general, one could safely assume that elements of the Turkish government were aware of my close collaboration with the movement.[78] I suspect that much of the harassment and attacks I received on my social media accounts after the publication of *The Humanity of Muhammad* were driven by "bot farms" orchestrated by Turkish intelligence services or entities working on behalf of the Muslim Brotherhood. This situation was severe enough that, in 2021, I met with a Houston-based FBI special agent to discuss what was happening. The agent agreed that my experience was a targeted campaign to reshape my public image and to squash the positive publicity I had been giving to interfaith dialogue and the Abraham Accords. This archetypal example of Orwellian manipulation, where reality is inverted to serve a specific political agenda, is a microcosm of how the "soft war" is waged and underscores the powerful, pervasive influence of subversive actors on the global chessboard.

Regarding the reasons behind the Gülen movement's cessation of communication with me following October 7, I can only hypothesize. It is possible that the movement found my firm public stance in support of Israel's war against Hamas to be problematic. While the loss of life in any war is tragic, I felt compelled to stand with Israelis, viewing Hamas

---

nates-gulen-religious-group-as-terrorists-idUSKCN0YM17F/.

78. Hakkı Taş, "Erdoğan and the Muslim Brotherhood: An Outside-in Approach to Turkish Foreign Policy in the Middle East," *Turkish Studies* 23 (2022): 772.

as an anti-Western and antisemitic Islamist regime akin to al-Qaeda, and Israel as a democracy, albeit an imperfect one, allied with the West.

Despite my continued commitment to interfaith dialogue and civic nation building—values I believe the Gülen movement still holds—any alliance we might have once had over this mutual goal is now "frozen." My interpretation of their response to October 7 is that they are effectively paralyzed. They are caught in the dangerous "no man's land" between two opposing sides on the battlefield, unable to align themselves fully with either Israel or the Palestinians. This is a perilous position. On the battlefield of both "soft" and "hard" wars, the consequences of inaction can prove equally fatal.

A similar but distinct set of dynamics emerged in my relationship with the Ahmadiyya movement following October 7. My connection with this community began during my PhD studies at Trinity College Dublin, when I read *The Wrong Kind of Muslim: An Untold Story of Persecution and Perseverance*, a book by Qasim Rashid, an Ahmadi American lawyer and "progressive" politician. Rashid's book spoke to me through his exploration of his community, which I was previously unfamiliar with, and his advocacy for interfaith dialogue and peaceful coexistence among Jews, Christians, and Muslims. Rashid followed in the footsteps of the movement's founder, Mirza Ghulam Ahmad, who advocated a "jihad of the pen"—a struggle through knowledge rather than violence. Over the next ten years, my connection with the movement blossomed. I befriended many of its leaders, spoke at its 2015 annual gathering, and hosted its national spokesperson, Harris Zafar, in my Rice University classes. I even had two private audiences with the movement's spiritual leader, Mirza Masroor Ahmad, whose presence and focus on peace and pluralism moved me. He even quoted my research on Muhammad's seventh-century relations with Christians in one of his speeches, which, to me, solidified a bond of "mutual respect."

Despite these positive developments, our amicable relationship encountered a significant fault line following October 7. In December 2023, I was invited to speak at an Ahmadiyya advocacy event in the House of Representatives that focused on "Middle East peace," particularly between Israel, Hamas, and the Palestinians.[79] To my dismay, the primary agenda in the days leading up to the event pivoted to advocating for a "ceasefire"—a position I found strategically unwise, as it would have prevented Israel from dismantling the terrorist organization on its border that had just executed horrific attacks. Despite Ahmadiyya media coverage stating otherwise, my speech intentionally refrained from calling for a ceasefire. In mingling with audience members following the conclusion of the event, I could sense the aggravation from several Ahmadis, signaling my divergence from their "pro-Palestinian" political positioning. For me, their stance, which aligned more with the Leftist-Islamist alliance than the U.S.-Israel alliance, was surprising given that Israel hosts an Ahmadiyya mosque in Haifa, a city in northern Israel, and upholds values like freedom of speech and freedom of religion, both of which are absent in the Gaza Strip and the wider Middle East. These human rights are denied to Ahmadis in Muslim-majority countries around the world, who categorize them as "non-Muslims" because of their beliefs on the finality of Muhammad's prophethood.

The Ahmadiyya Muslim movement's maneuvering in the "soft war" now includes labeling Israel as "genocidal" and the "oppressor," descriptions I have distanced myself from as they further the Leftist-Islamist cause. This positioning effectively mirrors the narratives produced by various Muslim Brotherhood–related entities in the civil sphere and in Congress. For example, Qasim Rashid, a self-identified "democratic socialist," has mocked "whiteness" on social media[80] and accused Israel

79. Faran Rabbani, "'Voices for Peace' Event Held on US Capitol Hill," *Weekly Al Hakam*, December 15, 2023, www.alhakam.org/voices-for-peace-event-held-on-us-capitol-hill/.

80. Qasim Rashid, X, posted dated June 3, 2025, x.com/QasimRashid/sta-

of committing a holocaust upon Palestinians, the kind of "counterhegemonic" narrative advanced by Rashida Tlaib, Ilhan Omar, and Alexandria Ocasio-Cortez.[81] In another Instagram post, he suggested that the Republican Party is "fascist," which I see as an egregious attempt to rewrite the definition of fascism.[82] This type of rhetoric is entrenched in "progressive" circles of Western politics, particularly in the United States and the United Kingdom, and aligns with the type of statements and arguments that come from the Muslim Brotherhood and other forces within the Leftist-Islamist alliance.

Returning to the hypothetical battlefield, it appears that the Gülen movement, the Ahmadiyya community, and I moved to different sides following October 7. From my perspective, Hizmet members have become effectively "silent," while the Ahmadis have moved closer to championing Marxist ideology and Islamist geopolitical goals. Despite these unfortunate realities, I have found new allies in other theaters of the "soft war," primarily through groups like Sharaka, which is working on the diplomatic front with issues pertaining to the Abraham Accords.

THE FINAL EQUATION: A REFLECTION ON TOLERATING THE INTOLERABLE

Albert Einstein, the German-American physicist and one of the most influential scientists of all time, is often quoted as saying, "I do not know with what weapons World War III will be fought, but World War IV will be fought with sticks and stones." Although this specific quote may be apocryphal, he often warned humanity of the dangers of nuclear war-

tus/1930089185706451205.

81. Qasim Rashid, "Holocaust," *Let's Address This with Qasim Rashid*, May 27, 2025, www.qasimrashid.com/p/holocaust.

82. Qasim Rashid, Instagram, posted dated July 24, 2025, www.instagram.com/p/DMfwd6wR7MG/.

fare, which could end human civilization and humankind as we know it. With no disrespect toward Einstein, I wonder whether World War III is already here in the form of a "non-nuclear" twenty-first-century style warfare that mirrors Sun Tzu's strategy laid out in *The Art of War*, with its focus on "deception" and "nondirect" conflict.

International forces are engaging the U.S.-Israel alliance in ways that suggest a state of subterranean warfare, where "soft power"—with its ideologically fueled "narratives"—is more powerful than "hard power"—with its bombs and bullets. "Soft power" can be as equally destructive as "hard power" because it infiltrates and attacks the system from the inside, in a "Trojan Horse" manner, instead of from outside a country's borders. This geopolitical dynamic points to another famous saying, "Every empire crumbles from within," meaning that the cause of an empire's collapse is not an external military threat, but rather internal decay, systemic breakdown of institutions, and cultural rot. As demonstrated throughout this book, the Leftist-Islamist alliance strategically uses the very infrastructures that are meant to protect and champion values like tolerance, free speech, and democratic governance. The attacks of Leftists and Islamists represent a calculated co-opting of Western institutions and values and a hijacking of narratives. This process of internal subversion, where a culture's values are turned against itself, is precisely what Orwell warned against. He cautioned that totalitarian regimes would use deception to shape public opinion and, in doing so, determine the fate of not just a nation but also the world.

Conclusion

THE PARADOX OF TOLERANCE: A STRATEGIC GUIDE TO DEFENDING THE WEST

As this book ends, one question looms above all others: how can the U.S.-Israel alliance, in particular, and the West more broadly offset the strategic maneuvers and "soft war" battlefield gains made by the Leftist-Islamist alliance? The preceding chapters have mapped the alliance's five components—foot soldiers on campus, ideological conditioning in academia, operational infrastructure in civil society, political rooks in Congress and elsewhere, and international kings and queens. The answer lies in the work of Karl Popper, the author of *The Open Society and Its Enemies*. Popper's book introduced the "tolerance of intolerance" paradox, one that is relevant to the "soft war."[1] His book sought to understand how the German public, composed of otherwise "good" people, could allow Adolf Hitler to ascend to power and commit such atrocities. Popper

1. Karl Popper, *The Open Society and Its Enemies: The Spell of Plato* (vol. 1) (Princeton, N.J.: Princeton University Press, 1966).

argued that German society's tolerance of the intolerant Nazis led to the destruction of tolerance itself. His main proposition was that tolerant individuals may tolerate intolerance, but the intolerant, conversely, will not extend the same courtesy, leading to a society devoid of tolerance. The paradox of tolerance reveals that a society, in its commitment to being "open," risks being devoured by the very forces it tolerates.

Popper's solution to this paradox asserted that to preserve a tolerant society, one must be "intolerant of intolerance." His strategy to counter intolerance stipulated that tolerant members of society should first engage with intolerant ideas through rational argument and civil public discourse. This strategy was expanded upon by John Rawls, the philosopher and author of *A Theory of Justice*, who posited that the principle of complete tolerance is superseded by a society's inherent right to "self-preservation." Rawls concurred with Popper that a tolerant society possesses the right to self-defense in extreme circumstances, adding the crucial condition that this right should be exercised only when the tolerant "sincerely and with reason" believe their own safety and liberty are genuinely imperiled.[2] This nuanced understanding of tolerance—where the embrace of liberty does not extend to allowing its own destruction—serves as a vital framework for analyzing the challenges posed by the Leftist-Islamist alliance, which often exploits the very tolerance it aims to dismantle. The foot soldiers, the ideological indoctrination, the operational infrastructure, the political vanguard, and the international patrons of this alliance all push boundaries that demand a critical reevaluation of tolerance for the preservation of Western values.

---

2. John Rawls, *A Theory of Justice* (Cambridge, Mass.: Belknap Press, 1971), 220.

CONFRONTING THE PARADOX: A BLUEPRINT FOR SELF-PRESERVATION

With this philosophical foundation in place, we can now translate Popper's theory into action across each front of the soft war. Being "intolerant of intolerance," as Popper urged, requires the West to establish clear boundaries to protect its civic culture. Tolerance is essential, and it must extend to a wide range of ideas and expressions. However, genuine tolerance also demands rational debate and respectful democratic civility as its foundation. The "red line" that marks the boundary of permissibility is crossed when individuals living in the West engage in actions that incite violence, disrupt institutions, and undermine bedrock principles of liberal democracy. As Rawls observed, the principle of self-preservation becomes legitimate and necessary when there is evidence-based belief that core liberties or public safety are endangered.

To borrow the famous historical phrase associated with Caesar's march on Rome—we have crossed the Rubicon. The West must not resort to censoring unpopular views, as doing so would betray its own foundational values. At the same time, it must become tougher on activities that threaten others or block their ability to exercise basic rights. This approach does not constitute censorship, despite claims to the contrary from the Leftist-Islamist alliance. Rather, it represents a critically important defense of the tolerant society's framework against those who exploit its openness to advance and impose their own intolerant agenda.

Western civilization's tolerance faces a challenge when radical students and their extreme ideologies exploit the university system's inherent openness. The actions and rhetoric of groups like SJP exemplify the dangers of unlimited tolerance that allows intolerance to flourish. The group's invocation of "free speech" is a strategic maneuver, justifying actions that, if left unchecked, could suppress the freedoms of others, lead to the breakdown of civil discourse, and result in direct attacks on Jewish students and their allies who reject antisemitism. Despite their antisemitism and revolutionary calls for violence, the "foot soldiers" are often tolerated, which undermines the principles of tolerance and pluralism that academic institutions claim to uphold.

To preserve a tolerant society, a distinction must be made. While rational debate is paramount and must be safeguarded, speech that incites violence or undermines the foundations of a tolerant society should not be accommodated. Universities must bear the responsibility of drawing a firm line between legitimate "free speech" and "hate speech" as demarcated by First Amendment principles.

The seeds of subversion extend beyond the "foot soldiers" to encompass academic curricula and university culture. The "ideological conditioning" on campuses and across society waters the seeds of radicalization, highlighting how Popper's "paradox" plays out. Marxist academics have worked to "control the narrative" by redefining racism, promoting cultural relativism, and reframing Western values as "problematic" and, in some cases, downright "evil." The dominance of theories like CRT, critical social justice, post-colonialism, Orientalism, and Islamophobia has created an environment where dissenting voices in the classroom and on campuses are marginalized, if not silenced, echoing Popper's concerns that a society's toleration undermines the very concept of tolerance.

In addition to clarifying their free speech codes, universities must fund and support initiatives that expose students to a range of intellectual and political viewpoints, including conservative and centrist perspectives, which are virtually nonexistent in the current academic climate. This counters ideological echo chambers, strengthens critical thinking, and makes students less susceptible to "indoctrination." Universities could strengthen requirements for courses on Western civilization, American civics, constitutional principles, classical philosophy, and the dangers of totalitarian ideologies like communism and Islamism. In doing so, students will gain an understanding of the values and institutions the alliance seeks to undermine, thereby protecting them from radical ideologies. What is more, academic departments, especially in the social sciences and humanities (where Marxism dominates), should be "de-politicized" to prioritize rigorous scholarship and open inquiry over partisan advocacy and ideological subversion. These principled stands are essential to prevent the very values that define Western civilization from being weaponized against it.

Popper's solution to these matters becomes paramount: the necessity for the tolerant to be intolerant of intolerance for self-preservation. Thankfully, Congress is acting as society's immune response by targeting organizations like SJP, AMP, CAIR, JVP, and TPF, including investigations into their finances and ties to rogue international actors. These organizations frame themselves as operating within civil society and utilize America's constitutional protections for nonprofits and rights to assembly and speech. While they frame themselves as civil rights organizations and humanitarian outlets, roles that a tolerant society is naturally inclined to support, their true agenda is far more radical. Their rhetoric, even when presented in the name of "social justice" or "anti-imperialism," is shown to be something much more sinister: anti-American, anti-capitalist, anti-democratic, anti-Israel, and anti-West. By exploiting the boundaries of tolerance, these groups are able to obfuscate their funding, orchestrate disruptive activism on campuses and American streets, and spread unchecked propaganda on social media with the support of foreign actors.

With regard to the "operational infrastructure" (the organizations and networks) of the Leftist-Islamist alliance, measures should be taken at the local, state, and national level to strengthen laws like the Foreign Agents Registration Act (FARA) to ensure full disclosure of nefarious foreign funding to nonprofit organizations as well as academic institutions. Stringent penalties should be imposed on noncompliance if the "money trail" reveals illegal activities or national security threats. Local, state, and national governmental entities should vigorously investigate any organizations that are suspected of providing financial, logistical, or ideological support to groups that promote terrorism. Adding to these measures, policymakers should do more to empower civil society organizations that promote dialogue, pluralism, and peacebuilding, "kryptonite" to the Leftist-Islamist alliance's divisive tactics. This demonstrates a Popperian approach—countering regressive intolerance with constructive tolerance.

Progressive politicians are actively aligning themselves with entities seeking to radically transform, if not eradicate, the very foundations of tolerance. By voting against the U.S.-Israel alliance and traditional Western values, promoting illiberalism, condoning antisemitism, justifying Hamas's terrorism, controlling discourse, and denying objective reality, these progressive politicians make genuine dialogue impossible. In the case of the Israel-Hamas conflict, their consistent pivoting to blaming Israel rather than Hamas leaves no room for nuance or compromise, a hallmark of an intolerant ideology that uses tolerance as a shield. This is a direct manifestation of Popper's concern—that unlimited tolerance allows the intolerant to gain power and subsequently erode the conditions that enable tolerance. Congress must continue, if not ramp up, its use of democratic legislative mechanisms to "check" these progressive pieces. The Democratic Party must also reel in the left flank of its party, as the progressive wing is increasingly emboldened and attractive to younger generations that have been subject to nearly unchecked ideological conditioning. In this way, the tolerant system can—per Popper and Rawls—push back from within the system itself.

Moreover, reforms in immigration policy, combined with the Democratic Party reining in its Marxist flank, are vital to addressing intolerance before it takes root in American society. Stricter attention to vetting is essential to ensure that immigrants align with core Western values, with particular emphasis on security and assimilation. Recent measures have advanced these objectives effectively. In January 2026, the U.S.

State Department paused the issuance of immigrant visas to nationals of 75 high-risk countries identified as posing elevated risks. This pause, effective January 21, 2026, builds directly on President Trump's Executive Order 14161 from January 2025, which prioritized national security through enhanced screening and vetting to protect the United States from foreign threats.

Furthermore, to promote the assimilation of immigrants, American institutions must revive the traditional "melting pot" model over the multicultural "salad bowl" approach. This can be achieved by requiring English proficiency exams and civic knowledge tests prior to admission and funding integration programs that emphasize shared civic values. These measures effectively counter the exploitation of the West's openness while fostering greater unity, all without eroding pluralism.

On the international relations front, the West must also continue forging positive engagements with less hostile Muslim countries. The Abraham Accords (2020 onward) endure despite the Gaza War. The U.A.E., Bahrain, Morocco, Kazakhstan, and Somaliland maintain ties with Israel, with the U.A.E. notably committed to strategic bridges via economic and technological partnerships. The Abraham Accords are not temporary; they are rooted in shared interests, proving that tactical alliances can foster lasting regional stability.

The "enemy of my enemy is my friend" dictum unites disparate international actors to wage a "soft war" against the West. This principle relates to Popper's warning that international forces exploit a society's tolerance by supporting groups and entities antithetical to Western democratic values. The alliance's primary weapon is not "hard power" but rather the "soft power" of ideologically fused narratives that hijack what is considered "tolerable" and "intolerable." This dynamic, likened to a "Trojan Horse," is, again, exactly what Popper warned about—that a tolerant society's own values, such as democratic governance, free speech, and societal openness, can be used against it to subvert institutions and create internal decay. With these realities in mind, the U.S.-Israel alliance's primary challenge is not an external military threat but rather the internal ideological subversion that exploits its commitment to tolerance. The U.S.-Israel alliance must maintain vigor while assessing how international forces can manipulate public opinion and encourage Westerners to view the West as the "problem" rather than the "solution." This requires a fundamental reevaluation of international alliances and the impact of globalization. Entities around the world should not be able to dictate the fate of Western civilization.

THE PAWN'S REBELLION: A KNIGHT'S MOVE ON THE CHESSBOARD

This book has served as both a sociological analysis of the Leftist-Islamist alliance and an autobiography of sorts of my experiences navigating it. My journey into what I now see as the "belly of the beast" has left me keenly aware of how easily a young Westerner and U.S. citizen can be drawn to radical ideologies. I am grateful that I was able to "see the light," even though this realization has come with the loss of friends and much unwanted public and private scrutiny. As the old saying goes, "The truth will set you free, but first, it will make you miserable."

My words may be a warning, but they also serve as a manual for navigating the "soft war" and reclaiming the truth. Moving forward, I hope this book can serve as a strategic "map" for the "kings" and "queens" of the U.S.-Israel alliance and broader West, as the "soft war" is far from over. This "soft" dynamic has forced us to confront the question of who we are—as Americans and Westerners. Our answer must be a renewed commitment to our own Enlightenment values of freedom, liberty, and equality. Still, we must also recognize Popper's paradox and refuse to tolerate our adversaries' intolerance.

Lastly, my own position on the metaphorical chessboard is that I was once a "pawn," easily moved by the flattering treatment of the Leftist-Islamist alliance. This book is my declaration that I am no longer a pawn, the chess piece that moves forward in a predictable, straight line. This journey from an "ally" to a "critic" represents the maneuvers of a "knight," the chess piece that moves unexpectedly, in a nonlinear trajectory, beyond the predictable patterns of conflict.

The soft war is far from over. Indeed, it is only just beginning. Its outcome will depend on whether Westerners choose to tolerate the intolerable or finally draw the line Popper and Rawls demanded. The well-being of the U.S.-Israel alliance—and of Western civilization itself—hinges on our commitment to defending the values that made us free. What will be your next move?

INDEX

About the Author

Craig Considine is the author of ten books on religion, ideology, and interfaith relations and an internationally recognized scholar on Islam. A Senior Lecturer in the Department of Sociology at Rice University since 2015, he specializes in the sociology of religion and the possibilities for constructive dialogue across Judaism, Christianity, and Islam. He has received fellowships from the Middle East Forum, the Jewish National Fund, and the Abraham Executive Academy, and he has lectured at the U.S. House of Representatives, Oxford University, NYU Abu Dhabi, and the Neue Synagogue Berlin. He lives in Houston, Texas.

www.ingramcontent.com/pod-product-compliance
Lightning Source LLC
LaVergne TN
LVHW041130070926
847404LV00049B/124